BEFORE

ACCORDING TO THE BIBLE AND SCIENCE

GENESIS

MIKE RITER

WESTBOW
PRESS®
A DIVISION OF THOMAS NELSON
& ZONDERVAN

WestBow Press books may be ordered through booksellers or by contacting:

WestBow Press
A Division of Thomas Nelson & Zondervan
1663 Liberty Drive
Bloomington, IN 47403
www.westbowpress.com
844-714-3454

Cover photo taken from Ernest R Lasher Memorial Park, Germantown,
NY. Is of the Hudson River and Catskill Mountains at sunset.

Scripture taken from the NEW AMERICAN STANDARD BIBLE (put a circle
'R'), Copyright ('c' in a circle) 1960, 1962, 1963, 1968, 1971, 1972, 1973, 1975, 1977,
1995 by The Lockman Foundation. Used by permission. www.Lockman.org.

ISBN: 978-1-6642-9887-3 (sc)
ISBN: 978-1-6642-9888-0 (e)

Library of Congress Control Number: 2023905813

Print information available on the last page.

WestBow Press rev. date: 04/28/2023

CONTENTS

PREFACE

Come along with me on an adventure into a world you've never seen or imagined! At times, though factual, it may seem unreal! Let us worship God together as we study how He prepared a place for our ancestors to live. Let us thank Him for all the things He made for us. "This is the day that The Lord has made. Let us rejoice and be glad in it." (Psalm 118:24). When Abraham thought he was sacrificing the son he loved, he told little Isaac, "We will go yonder and worship." (Genesis 22:5). How could he consider this, the first mention of worship in The Bible, to be an occasion that called for worship? Simply because, at this point in his life-relationship with God, he saw everything as a reason to worship. Besides, he thought God would raise Isaac from the dead (Hebrews 11:17-19). Regardless, Abraham had learned "God works all things for the good of those who love Him and are called according to His purpose." (Romans 8:28). So he always praised and thanked God.

Job experienced some of the worst news any person could! In a few minutes he learned he lost all of his valuable animals and his house blew down, killing his children! Of course he was grief-stricken! He "arose, tore his robe, shaved his head, fell to the ground and worshipped! He said, 'Yahweh gave and Yahweh has taken away! Blessed be the name of Yahweh!'" (Job 2:20-21). Oh how God has blessed us with such a wonderful planet to live on! As far as anyone knows, the rest of the physical universe is hostile! There are unimaginably dangerous things out there, including black holes, supernovas and pulsars! They are all too far away to harm us. God has placed our planet in the "Goldilocks zone," where everything is just right. He has given us sunshine, clouds, rain, air to breathe, wind to cool us, green grass, blue sky, and a wide variety of delicious and nutricious foods to eat. We are like Thoreau's, "delicate flowers," that grew unharmed, "Between the horses' path and the wheel track."

We should see ourselves as a raindrop, securely-held in the vast ocean of God's love!

INTRODUCTION

In order to find out what The Bible teaches happened before the Genesis restoration/revealing/arraying, we must determine what happened in Genesis One! What the Bible and science combine to tell us happened BEFORE GENESIS!

Before we get into Creation vs. Evolution, God vs. Atheism, Young Earth Creationism (YEC) vs. Ancient Earth Creationism (AEC), I will set the stage. Throughout, I will use the NEW AMERICAN STANDARD BIBLE (1995), with my slight changes. I put it in my own words, where I think I can make what is said clearer. I will reveal where I'm coming from and why. I believe in clear, no-nonsense science and Biblical teachings. We must not accept, in any area, by anyone, what the Apostle Peter called, "Cleverly devised fables" (II Peter 1:16). We must deal in solid facts just as Jesus and His Prophets and Apostles always did. The Apostle Paul said, "Each person must be fully convinced in his own mind." (Romans 14:5b). We cannot be "fully convinced" in any sort of informed way, unless we've seen the intricate details of various beliefs including our own. We arrive at truth "line upon line, here a little, there a little." (Isaiah 28:10b). If we only listen to those we agree with, the truth or parts of it, likely will allude us. We must remember the words of Solomon: "The first to state his case seems right, until another comes and disputes him." (Proverbs 18:17). World famous skeptic, Michael Shermer, has correctly stated, "Smart people are better at making up believable clever arguments and reasons." Facts must be explained--not explained-away. When their research is superior in a given area, I learn from and quote people I disagree with on major points. Michael Shermer's, "The Believing Brain" speaks of brains that accept illogical or highly unlikely beliefs that promote a certain hypothesis. I look for solid probabilities. I like to ask, "What are the chances …?" I do not accept arguments that are logically-incoherent! I've been at this for over 55 years and I think I know when someone is trying to pull the wool over my eyes. I'm not a recognized player in this debate and am fine with it if I never become one, as long as my message reaches those God has planned to read it. I'm similar to Amos, who told Amaziah, "I am not a prophet, nor am I the son of a prophet; for I am a herdsman and a grower of sycamore figs. But the Lord took me from following the flock and the Lord told me, 'Go prophesy to My people Israel.'" (Amos 7:14-15). I do not relish proving others wrong. That's the toughest part of this study! I hate to contradict your favorite Bible teacher. If you are a student or a teacher, maybe you'll change some of your views. Of course I'm trying to change minds or I wouldn't be writing! In any event, at least I hope I give you all some new facts to consider. I would be remiss to know what I know and not share it. I believe, by the grace of God, I have some important things to say! Am I uniquely qualified to tackle this subject? You be the judge! Having said all of this, I don't care who you are, you're a better person than I. That's enough said!

ONE

Things Are Often Not As They Seem To Be
There Are Biblical Examples Of Mistaken Beliefs
Humbly Admit You May Wrong On Given Subjects
(Always Read And Listen Carefully)

THE ONLY PEOPLE WHO BELIEVE CORRECTLY, ARE THOSE WHO'VE changed their minds a number of times. New facts forced me to admit I was wrong and adjust my belief-system many times! The Bible gives us many examples of people who were forced to change their views on highly-important topics, including what they were really like in their hearts! They had to concede that their own judgments and abilities were far different from what they had envisioned! The Disciples had to learn to pay close attention to Jesus. For example, they thought Jesus told Peter, John the beloved disciple would still be on Earth when He returned, but He only said, "If I want him to remain until I come, what is that to you? You follow Me!" (John 21:21-23). Peter and the other disciples thought they were brave and reliable. Jesus told them, "You will fall away," and "before the rooster crows twice, you will deny Me three times," "But Peter kept insisting, 'Even if I have to die with You, I will not deny you!' And they were all saying the same thing too." Then after Jesus poured out His soul in prayer in the Garden of Gethsemane, He found the disciples asleep, unable to pray with Him, at this, one of history's greatest hours! He said to Peter, "Simon, are you asleep? Could you not watch for one hour? Keep watching and praying that you may not come into temptation; the spirit is willing, but the flesh is weak." After finding them asleep two more times He told them, "Are you still sleeping and resting? It is enough; the hour has come! Behold, the Son of Man (His favorite term when referring to Himself), is being betrayed into the hands of sinners." Peter then denied Jesus three times before a "servant-girl," and "Immediately a rooster crowed a second time. And Peter remembered how Jesus had told him, 'Before the rooster crows twice, you will deny Me three times.' And he began to weep bitterly." (Mark 14:27-72). We all need our rest and sleep, but ask yourself, "Am I sleeping when I should be awake and praying, and/ or resting when I should be busy serving God?" Peter and the other disciples had to fail and fall terribly in order to learn that Jesus was right, "I am the vine, you are the branches; he who abides in Me and I in him, he bears much fruit, for apart from Me you cannot do anything right." (John 15:5).

James told his fellow Jews, "You believe in one God! Good for you! The demons also believe and tremble!" (James 2:19). James is letting them know, they are wrong to consider it enough to believe God exists! He even said, in a way, demons are ahead of you because, at least they know enough to tremble! Now it's true, "he who comes to God, must believe that He exists and He is the rewarder of those who seek Him." (Hebrews 11:6). But we are to know God and not just know about Him. Do you know Him? Do you know Him intimately? Do you love Him? Do you love Him deeply, with every fiber of your being? All of us are in darkness until we meet Jesus through His word. We must pray earnestly and listen to sermons and/or read books of sermons. Human testimony is vital because, the human element adds power to God's word. Otherwise, God would use angels or write the Gospel in the sky! When the Apostles testified and preached the Old Testament concerning Jesus, it had a much deeper and more powerful effect on the hearers than if they simply read it! That is not to say we are not to read and memorize what we can each day in both Testaments. When Billy Graham travelled the world, he met people who memorized the entire Bible! Oh how far off we are to own Bibles and not open them day after day, as if there are more important things to do!

This brings us to the question Billy Graham said he was most often asked: "How can I know I'm a Christian?" In a way, there's no easy answer! The short simple answer is: "If you have met Jesus inwardly and have given Him your heart, most likely weeping over your sins and wanting to live a different life with Him in control, then you are a Christian!" You will be a weak Christian at first, but don't be discouraged! Jesus knows you begin as a "baby in Christ," needing to grow! The sad thing is, after several years, many have hardly grown at all! The world is not impressed by churches full of weak Christians! Those outside the true Church, are said to be, "those who do not know God" (I Thessalonians 1:8).

THE BLIND, DECIEVED CALLED-OUT-BELIEVERS AT LOADICEA

The Book of Revelation was originally written to seven called-out-assemblies (ekklesias), "churches." The most difficult one to explain prophetically, is Laodicea. Though each of the seven letters in Revelation 2 and 3, was written to an actual church in Asia Minor, yet each is also a prophecy, as the entire Book is called such in 1:3. Toward the end of all seven letters, we find: "He who has an ear, let him hear what the Spirit says to the churches" (plural). That is because what is mainly aimed at each individual assembly, applies to some in all of the other six assemblies and to all called-out-assemblies that would ever exist. So when the believers in these assemblies are rebuked, we must not say, "Oh how awful they were," without considering our own faults! The final four types of assemblies, will remain until the end of the age. They are "Thyatira" (Catholics); "Sardis" (Protestants); "Philadelphia" (the brethren movement); and "Laodicea," which the brilliant scholar, Watchman Nee taught, "was the proud among the brethren movement." Just as Protestantism came out of Catholicism and the brethren came out of Protestantism, so 'the proud brethren (Laodicea)," came out of the "brotherly love" brethren. What is it that caused this called-out-assembly at Laodicea to be so proud? History tells us the brethren (and they never capitalized it), knew the Bible better than anyone else, by far! From their books I have, I can confirm that fact. For a long time they were all very humble! When they wrote books, it was normal to only use two initials and their last name," i.e." J. N. Darby. I'm reading an incredible book by Charles Henry Mackintosh, "THE MISCELLANEOUS WRITINGS of C. H. M." (not even a last name!).

Before I get into Laodicia, I will spend a few words on Thyatira. The internet has an ongoing debate: "Are there true born-again Christians in the Catholic Church?" To my dismay, there are highly-respected Bible-scholars who, due to certain Catholic-beliefs and practices, don't think there are. In the history of Catholicism, there have been those who knew Jesus Christ in a deep way, and there still are now. I recommend reading EXPERIENCING THE DEPTHS OF JESUS CHRIST by Jeanne Guyon. I see some Catholics as those who are the opposite of 2 Timothy 3:5, so they might not hold the correct "form of Godliness," but proclaim, in several ways, "its power." Not only are there born-again Catholics, but there are also "overcomers" (Rev. 2:26). Catholic priests lead the way in casting out demons and speak out strongly against killing unborn babies! Catholics were a great help during Billy Graham Crusades. Jesus gives these overcomers, "the morning star" (Rev. 2:28). That's because many practice communing with Christ before dawn and often see Venus, "the morning star." Those who are hard on Catholics concerning their "form of Godliness," are forgetting the most important thing: "Yahweh looks deep into the heart" (1 Samuel 16:7). What does He see in our hearts?

So now we come to the letter to the called-out-assembly at Laodicea (Rev. 3:14-22). Having come out from "the brethren," their Bible knowledge was unsurpassed! There were no mistakes in their doctrines, and they knew it! John says, "To the messenger of the called-out-assembly in Laodicea write." Many Bibles have "angel" instead of "messenger," but that is an unlikely translation. In Philippians 2:25, we find a human "messenger" named "Epaphroditus," that the Apostle Paul sent to the Philippians. Apparently a messenger, like Epaphroditus, read this letter aloud to the assembly. These believers, knowing so much, knew John, being close to Jesus, was not going to make a mistake in what he said. They leaned forward in their seats, in great anticipation of all the praise Jesus was about to shower them with through the Apostle John. There's a hush as the messenger speaks: "The Amen, the Faithful and True Witness, the Beginning of the creation of God, says this: 'I know your deeds, that you are neither cold nor hot: I wish that you were cold or hot. So because you are lukewarm and neither hot nor cold, I will spit you out of My mouth!'" The Loadiceans are hanging their heads in total bafflement! Laodicea didn't have wells. The water was piped in from miles away and was often a nasty lukewarm, causing the drinker to spit it out! So they clearly knew what Jesus was saying! But they didn't understand why He said it? The messenger continued, "Because you say, 'I am rich, and have become wealthy and have need of nothing!'" Once we think we've arrived, thinking we're spiritually rich, having no needs, we have already fallen badly! Right here is the greatest problem the modern church has! WE ARE BLIND TO OUR OWN SPIRITUAL CONDITION! WE HAVE NO IDEA WHAT WE ARE REALLY LIKE! WE DON'T REALIZE THAT WE ARE UNRELIABLE, SELF-SEEKING, PLEASURE-LOVING, TIME-WASTING AND ROTTEN-TO-THE-CORE! Why is it we don't seek God with all our hearts? Why is it we don't seek God early every morning, to get our day off to a proper start with Bible reading and communion with Jesus? Simply because we think we are already fine! Why do our days go haywire, being on edge, with self-seeking, sour-impatient personalities? Because we don't see that we can't get by without Jesus! We think it's fine to start our days without prayer, praise, thanksgiving and Bible-reading! So the messenger continues: "and you do not know that you are wretched and miserable and poor and blind and naked." Jesus said "I know," and "you do not know." We are "wretched" to the point where our only hope is: "I have been crucified with Christ: and it is no longer I who live, but Christ lives in me. And the life which I now live in the body, I live by the faith of the Son of God." (Galatians 2:20). Young's Literal Translation says, "in the faith I live of the Son of God" (Gal. 2:20b). Paul didn't even live by his own faith, but by Christ's! And "miserable!" I hope by now we all know ourselves well enough, so I don't have to comment on our miserableness! And "poor," without Christ"s riches; and "blind," without Christ's light; and "naked," without being clothed in Christ's righteousness! I want to talk further concerning the "light" we need! Psalm 36:10 says, "For with You is the fountain of life. In Your light we see light." We are not to search our hearts ourselves! That's valueless! David said, "Search me O God and know my heart! Try me and know my anxious thoughts, and see if there is any hurtful way in me! And lead me in the everlasting way." (Psalm 139:23-24). Let God show us and teach us!

Jesus doesn't rebuke them without telling the Laodiceans how to solve their problems and so He continues, "I advise you to buy from Me gold refined by fire so that you may become rich, and white garments so that you may clothe yourself, and the shame of your nakedness will not be revealed; and eyeslave to anoint your eyes so that you may see" (Laodecia was known for its eyeslave). Jesus says, "Buy from Me," because you must pay the price by rising early every morning to spend time in prayer, praise and Bible-reading. Only then can you become spiritually-rich, insightful and refined.

Jesus, knowing how easily His church doubts His love for them after a harsh rebuke, had to set the record straight! Even as He rebuked them, His love for them burned intensely! He couldn't hold it back any longer, and said, "Those whom I love, I reprove and discipline; be zealous therefore and repent. Behold I stand at the door and knock; if anyone hears My voice and opens the door, I will come in to him and will dine with him, and he with Me." In Luke 11:9 Jesus told

His Disciples, "knock and it will be opened to you," but here His love burned so brightly and intensely that He couldn't wait for the Laodiceans to knock, and so He knocked first! The main points of this letter was for Jesus to let His called-out-ones know how much they needed Him and how deeply He loved them!

THE ON-TOP-OF DEAD-BONES PROBLEM

It's been said, Genesis One cannot be about a restoration of a previously-judged civilization because, God wouldn't call a new-world built on the buried-bones of dead-animals,"very good!" My response: Just because dead-bones are buried beneath, doesn't mean God wouldn't call His restored local-land, with its new plants and animals, "very good!" After all, there will be trillions of more bones buried when God's 1,000-year, kingdom-age arrives! Can anyone say, God's Kingdom on Earth won't be, "very good?" (Rev. 20:4-6, Matt. 26:29, Luke 11:2).

TWO

The Cosmos Jesus And The Apostles Spoke Of
(Called Out Of What?)

THE GREEK WORD "EKKLESIA" TRANSLATED "CHURCH," MEANS, "called-out-ones." But called out of what? The answer is: "the cosmos." Look in any dictionary and you'll see many words have several meanings. This is true of the Greek word "cosmos." Although it is one of its meanings, Jesus isn't speaking of Carl Sagon's "cosmos," (physical Universe),when He speaks of the "cosmos" He calls His church out of. Rather He refers to "Satan's-system-of-beliefs, ways-of-living, things that may attract us and distract us, and the people in his kingdom, with their darkened-minds." Jesus called the devil, "the ruler of this cosmos" (John 12:31). When the devil tempted Jesus by offering Him "all the kingdoms of the cosmos and their glory," Jesus didn't say, "they're not yours to give," but replied, "Go Satan! For it is written, 'You shall worship the Lord your God, and only serve Him.'" (Matt. 4:10). We must be careful not to allow worldly-education,things or entertainment to ruin our minds and lives! We must realize "the wisdom of this cosmos is foolishness" (1 Cor. 3:19). "Do not love the cosmos, nor the things of the cosmos. If anyone loves the cosmos, the love of the Father is not in him. For all that is in the cosmos; the lust of the flesh, the lust of the eyes, and the boastful pride of life, is not of the Father, but is from the cosmos. The cosmos is passing away and its lusts; but the one who does the will of God lives forever." (1 John 2: 15-17).

In these last days, the cosmos will unite and expand! That means there will be a one-world government with the devil and his Antichrist as its rulers. This will be a somewhat overturning of what God did at the Tower of Babel, where He turned the one-original-cosmos-language into many languages so the people He scattered to various places could not understand those in other places. (Genesis 11:1-9) When everyone in the cosmos understands the others, they unite against the God. A Psalmist said, "Why are the nations (O. T. cosmos), in an raging-uproar and the peoples devising a vain thing? The kings of the Earth take their stand, and the rulers plan together against Yahweh and His anointed (Hebrew, mahsheeagh) (Psalm 2:1-2). "Anointed" here refers to Yahweh's people! Isaiah 45:1 says, "Thus says Yahweh to Cyrus His anointed, whom I have taken by the right hand." Obedient Old-Testament-Jews and New-Testament-Christians are His anointed (Habakkuk 3:13; 1John 2:20, 27). However, it is also true that Yahweh/Jesus is Himself referred to by Daniel as "The Messiah" (Mahsheeagh) "Anointed One" (Dan. 9:25-26).

Jesus told His disciples, "If the cosmos hates you, you know that it hated Me before you! If you were of the cosmos, the cosmos would love its own; but because you are not of the cosmos, but I chose you out of the cosmos, the cosmos hates you!" (John 15:18-19).

Now this doesn't mean we are not to use the cosmos at all! The Apostle Paul said it was okay to "use the cosmos," but "not make full use of it; for the form of this cosmos is passing away" (1Corinthians 7:31). God refuses to use those who are afraid of the cosmos-people. There were 32,000 in Gideon's army. God told him, "Whoever is afraid-and-trembling, let him return and depart from Mount Gilead." "So 22,000 people returned." God further tested the 10,000 that remained, "So Yaweh said to Gideon, You shall separate everyone who laps the water with his tongue as a dog laps, as well as everyone who kneels to drink. Now the number of those who lapped, putting their hands to their mouth, was 300 men; but the rest of the people kneeled to drink water. Yaweh said to Gideon, 'I will deliver you with the 300 who lapped'" (Judges 7:1-7).

How is it God chose to only use 300 out of 32,000? In his Commentary (p.343), Matthew Henry said, "Cowards would be as likely as any, after the victory, to take the honour of it from God, and therefore God would not do them the honour to employ them in it. Fearful and faint-hearted-people are not fit to be employed for God; and, among those that are enlisted under the banner of Christ, there are more than we think there are." Jesus told His disciples, "I say to you My friends, do not be afraid of those who kill the body and after that have no more that they can do. But I will warn you Whom to fear: fear the One Who, after He has killed, has authority to cast into Gehenna-fire; yes, I tell you, fear Him!" (Luke 12:4-5).

Now why did God refuse to use the 9,700 who got down on their knees to drink? To get on their knees to drink, shows they were people who were indulging themselves at a time when they should've shown restraint and concentrated on being alert and ready to serve! On the other hand, in his commentary (p. 246), Francis Davidson said, "those who conveyed water from the spring to their mouths in their cupped hands would be able to keep a wary eye open for sudden attack." I remember Watchman Nee saying in a book, "Those who got down on their knees, weren't ready because they had to take their backpacks off!" Will we serve God with all our hearts! Are we ready?

The 300 were humble men who wanted to please God instead of themselves! Humility doesn't equal timidity. It means to live without considering your own life precious to yourself (Acts 20:24). These men were disciples of Yahweh-their-God! When Yahweh became Jesus, He taught unless you hate your life, you "cannot be My disciple" (Luke 14:26). To hate your life is not to get side-tracked by pleasures. It's a great privilege to serve God. It's an extreme privilege to suffer and/or die for Christ's sake. Not everyone has the love for God He requires! After being beaten and jailed for preaching Christ, the Apostles were, "rejoicing that they had been considered worthy to suffer shame for His name." (Acts 5:18, 40-41).

The 300 determined to serve God, come what may! They wanted to obey and please God, with the attitude: "If I die, I die!" When Nebuchadnezzar threatened to throw three Hebrew men "into the midst of a furnace-of-blazing-fire," if they didn't "worship the golden-image" he set up, they said, "If it be, our God Whom we serve is able to deliver us from the furnace-of-blazing-fire; and He will deliver us out of your hand, O king. But if not, let it be known to you O king, that we are not going to serve your gods or worship the golden-image that you have set up." (Daniel 3:5-6, 17-18). The furnace was heated "seven-times more than it was usually heated," so that it, "killed those men" who "threw them in the furnace-of-blazing-fire." (3:19-23). Then "Nebuchadnezzar the king was astonished and stood up quickly," and said, "Look! I see four men loosed, walking in the midst of the fire without harm, and the fourth is like the son of gods" (3:24-25). He admitted, "There is no other god who is able to deliver in this way." (3:29).

In the Old Testament, Jesus Christ was called "Yahweh," and looked like a glorified man or an angel (a little above humans--Hebrews 2:7). The personage Jacob wrestled with one night, was referred to as "a man," "an angel" and "Yahweh" (Hosea 12:4-5, Genesis 32:24). There's no doubt Yahweh became Jesus because Yahweh said, "they will gaze upon Me Whom they have pierced" (Zechariah 12:1-10). When Jesus said, "Before Abraham was born, 'I Am'" "they picked up stones to throw at Him." (John 8:58-59). They knew He was calling Himself Yahweh! The reason we look like Him is because we're made in His image. (Genesis 1:26-27). "Then God "Eloheem" (plural) said, 'Let Us" (plural) "make man in Our" (plural) "image'" (singular). When the Trinity said, "Let Us make man in Our image," they referred only to Yahweh's image because neither the Father nor the Holy Spirit have an image, but are Spirits. Jesus said, "God is Spirit, and those who worship Him, must worship in spirit and truth." (John 4:24).

At the same time, of course, Jesus-the-Creator, is above-all-angels, and so Hebrews 1:6 says, "Let all of the angels of God worship Him." And again, quoting Psalm 110:1, Hebrews 1:13 asks; "But to which of the angels has He ever said, 'Sit at My right hand until I make Your enemies a footstool for your feet?'" This is the same Lord that is said to have "laid the foundations of the Earth," "And the heavens are the works of Your hands." (Hebrews 1:10).

WE CANNOT GET FROM THE DEVIL'S KINGDOM TO THE KINGDOM OF GOD ON OUR OWN MERITS

We must not remain in the Devil's kingdom (cosmos). In your-brief-life, you must escape! "The whole-cosmos lies in the grip of the evil-one." (1John 5:19). "With gentleness, correcting those who are in opposition, if perhaps God may grant them repentance, leading to the knowledge of the truth, and they may come to their senses from the snare of the Devil, having been held captive by him to do his will." (2 Timothy 2:25-26). We must escape! But, "How will we escape if we neglect so-great-a-salvation?" (Hebrews 2:3). How can we obtain this "so-great-a-salvation?" Speaking of Jesus Christ, Acts 4:12 says: "there is salvation in no one else: for there is no other name under heaven that has been given among men by which we must be saved." Jesus said, "I Am the Way, the Truth and the Life; no one comes to the Father but through Me." (John 14:6).

We need this great-salvation that is found only in Jesus Christ, because we have no way to attain it in any other way! Oh yes! Solomon said, "There's a way that seems right to a man, but it ends in death." (Proverbs 14:12). How can we save ourselves by our own wisdom, when Jeremiah said, "Nor is it in man who walks to direct his steps." (Jer. 10:23). And we have no way in ourselves to find out how sinful we really are! Jeremiah further stated: "The heart is deceitful beyond everything else and desperately wicked! Who can know it? I Yahweh search the heart and test the mind." (Jer. 17:9-10).

Maybe you have some idea concerning how evil you are? But you're nowhere near knowing your-true-condition! What you are really like! We all begin in darkness! Jesus said, "I Am the Light of the cosmos." (John 8:12). Matthew said, "The people who were sitting in darkness saw a Great Light, and those who were sitting in the land and shadow of death, upon them a light dawned." (Matt. 4:15-16 and Isaiah 9:2). We all are or have been, "sitting in darkness," and in "the valley of the shadow of death." (Psalm 23:4).

So maybe you think you're good enough? James said, "Whoever keeps the whole law and yet stumbles in one point, he is guilty of all." (Ja. 2:10). Jesus said, "Make friends quickly with your opponent at law while you are with him on the way, so that your opponent may not hand you over to the judge, and the judge to the officer, and you be thrown into prison. Truly I say to you, you will not come out of there until you have paid up the last cent." (Matt. 5:25-26). Oh how we need to apologize quickly to anyone we've wronged--before we or they die and it's too late! Even when we're on the right side of an argument, we should have the good-grace to apologize anyway! These words show how God thinks, but are actually only meant for Christians because the cosmos cannot "have paid off the last cent." Christians who think they can live any way they want and not be punished, have a bad-surprise-coming! There are people who've gone to Hades and saw Christians who lived loose lives, in cages of fire among worms, saying, "Why am I here?" "Until you've paid the last cent!" Three times Jesus told us to fear being cast into Gehenna (a place representing lower Hades), "where their worm does not die and the fire is not quenched" (Luke 9:43-49). Gehenna was the "Valley of Hinnom," where there were "ever-burning fires" of "all sorts of putrefying-matter." (The New Unger's Bible Dictionary, p. 462). Tertullian (c. 205, W, 5.174), spoke of "the lowest depths of Tartarus ... the prison of infernal punishments." (A Dictionary of Early Christian beliefs p. 637). On pages 637-8 Hippolytus said, "By means of this knowledge, you will escape the approaching threat of the fire of judgment and the black scenery of gloomy Tartarus, where a beam from the radiant voice of the Word never shines." (c.225, W, 5.153). In The Bible, only Peter speaks of Tartarus: "For if God did not spare angels when they sinned, but cast them into Tartarus and committed them to pits of darkness reserved for judgment." (2 Peter 2:4).

Jesus said, "Everyone who looks on a woman with lust for her has already committed adultery with her in his heart." (Matt. 5:28). James said, "And if it is with difficulty that the righteous is saved, what will become of the Godless man and the sinner" (Ja. 4:18). Jesus said, "No one is good except God alone." (Mark 10:18). There's one huge mistake the people of the Devil's-cosmos, and carnal-Christians make--they live-independently-of-God! They do not seek Him, to know what to do and how to live! Jesus told the religiou-leaders of His day, "You are those who justify yourselves before men, but God knows your hearts; for that which is highly esteemed among men is detestable in the eyes of God." (Luke 16:15). In addition, Isaiah said, "For all of us have become like one who is unclean, and all of our righteous deeds are like filthy menstrual rags. And all of us wither like a leaf, and our iniquities, like the wind, carry us away." (Isa. 64:6).

The Apostle Paul said, "Rejoice always, pray without ceasing; in everything give thanks,; for this is God's will for you in Christ Jesus" (1 Thessalonians 5:16-18).

THREE

How Can We Get From The Devil's Cosmos Into The Kingdom Of God?

HEBREWS 11:6 SAYS, "AND WITHOUT FAITH IT IS IMPOSSIBLE TO please, for he who comes to God must believe that He exists and He is the rewarder of those who seek Him." Yahweh told Jeremiah to tell the residents of Jerusalem, "For I know the plans I have for you, declares Yahweh; plans for welfare and not for calamity. To give you a future and a hope. Then you will call upon Me and come and pray to Me, and I will listen to you. You will seek Me and find Me when you search for Me with all your heart." (Jer 29:11-13). The Athenians and the strangers at the Areopagus "used to spend their time in nothing other than telling or hearing something new." (Acts 17:21-22). So the Apostle Paul, with love for them burning in his heart, told them, "The God who made the world and all things in it ... made from one every nation of mankind to live on all the face of the Earth, having determined appointed times and the boundaries of their habitation. That they would seek God, if perhaps they may grope for Him and find Him, though He is not far from each one of us." (Acts 17:24-27). Paul said, "Therefore having overlooked the times of ignorance, God is now declaring to men that all everywhere should repent, because He has fixed a day in which He will judge the world in righteousness through a man He has raised from the dead" (Acts 17:30-31). The results were: "Now when they heard of the resurrection of the dead, some began to sneer, but others said, 'We shall hear you again concerning this.' So Paul went out of their midst. But some men joined him and believed, among whom were Dionysius and Areopagite and a woman named Damaris and others with them." (Acts 17:32-34).

Those who believed, sensed God and His love in their hearts! What does it mean to seek Him and find Him? And what will happen to us? The Apostle Paul told the-called-out-ones at Ephesus, "And you were dead in your trespasses and sins in which you walked according to the-course-of-this-cosmos; according to the prince of the power of the air; of the spirit that is now working in the sons of disobedience. Among them we too all formerly-lived in the lusts-of-our-flesh, indulging the desires of the flesh and of the mind, and were by nature children-of-wrath, just as the rest But God being rich-in-mercy, because of His great-love with which He loved us, even when we were dead in our transgressions, made us alive-together-with-Christ. By Grace you have been saved and raised up with Him and seated with Him in the heavenlies in Christ Jesus. For by grace you have been saved through faith; and that not of yourselves--it is the gift of God! Not as a result of deeds, so no one may boast." (Ephesians 2:1-9). You cannot justify yourself, as if, apart-from-God, the good you did or the sins you didn't commit will ultimately-matter, if you're still in the Devil's kingdom!! Comparing yourself with others, like the Pharisee did, will not get you anywhere no matter how careful you are! Jesus is only One that provides an escape!

HOW DID JESUS BECOME THE WAY TO THE GOD THE FATHER?

FOUR

"Without Shedding Of Blood There Is No Forgiveness"
(Hebrews 9:22)

JOSEPHUS ESTIMATES THAT 250,000 LAMBS WERE SLAUGHTERED IN Jerusalem on the 14th of the Jewish month of Nisan, with only a few thousand sacrificed in the Temple (Jewish Wars, Book IV. Chapter 9 Section 3). According to Harold W. Hoehner, the 14th fell on Friday in AD 33, when Jesus was crucified. (Chronological Aspects Of The Life OF Christ, pp. 103-105). So while Jesus, the Lamb of God was dying, so were 250,000 lambs. At the moment He died, "the veil of the Temple was torn in two from top to bottom and the earth shook and the rocks were split." "And many of the bodies of the dead saints ... were raised." (Matt. 27:51-52). "the centurion, and those who were with him keeping guard over Jesus, when they saw the earthquake and the things that were happening, became very frightened and said, 'Truly this was the Son of God!" (27:54).

The very first sins, by Adam and Eve, demanded an-animal-sacrifice, as shown by the fact that, "Yahweh Eloheem made garments of skin for Adam and his wife and clothed them." (Gen 3:21). Why must innocent animals be sacrificed? God in His wisdom, found a way to reconcile people to Himself. "For it was the Father's good pleasure for all the fullness to dwell in Him, and through Him to reconcile all things to Himself, having made peace through the blood of His cross" (Colossians 1:19-20). After all the, "life of all flesh is in its blood"

(Leviticus 17:14). But the only thing Old Testament sacrifices could do was to have those who sacrificed trust in the future-sacrifice of God's Son. Hebrews 10:4 says: "For it is impossible for the blood of bulls and goats to take away sins." "But He having offered one sacrifice for sins for all time, sat down at the right hand of God." (Hebrews 10:12).

All of our sins; our nasty words, evil lustful thoughts, horrific deeds and even our self-exalting-good-deeds, are like putrid-garbage on the-sheet-of-our-hearts! No matter how we try or what we do, we cannot erase them! But when we realize the veil has been torn, so we can approach God and trust Christ, calling on Him in faith; His shed blood washes all of our sins off of the sheet of our hearts! Call on Him now! Become a member of the true church! Become born again, called-out-of-Satan's-cosmos, to serve-the-living-God! May God help you to do it!

You can tell you're a Christian when you don't just know about God, but when you also know Him! 2 Thessalonians 1:8, speaks of "those who do not know God and those who do not obey the Gospel of our Lord Jesus."

BAPTISM BURRIES OUR OLD COSMOS AND TELLS IT WE NO LONGER BELONG TO IT

In Hindu countries to this very day, when someone is baptized, they become outcasts and are often beaten! And not long ago, there could not be a church in Hindu countries because, as soon as anyone was baptized, they were killed. Christians think the order should be: 1. Believe. 2. Be saved. And 3. Be baptized! Eternal life comes through faith alone! But that's not what Jesus talks about here! He said, "He who has believed and has been baptized shall be saved." (Luke 16:16). In order to understand why the order is this way, we must answer the question, "saved from what?" This is not about being saved from the-Eternal-Lake-of-Fire and obtaining eternal-life, where trusting-faith is what is needed (John 3:16). What Jesus is saying here is that baptism saves us from the cosmos! When we are tempted to enjoy-forbidden-cosmos-pleasures, once baptized, we can say, "I am dead and buried and I trust my baptism has delivered (saved) me from the cosmos, for I belong to Jesus. I will not go my own way; but His way!" We should not even look back at our old desires and way of life! That's why Jesus warned us, "Remember Lot's wife!" (Luke 17:32, Genesis 19:26).

I did not plan to say any of the above concerning the cosmos! It took me there! The reason I brought the subject up was to show that "sin and death happened more than once BEFORE GENESIS!" The teaching I'm trying to debunk says: "There cannot be death in the world until Adam sinned. Therefore all of the fossils found on Earth are from animals that died after Adam sinned" (Romans 5:12). But if sin and death only entered "the-Devil's-new-system," with plenty of both already being on the planet Earth before Adam sinned, then the Romans 5:12 argument that sin and death weren't here BEFORE GENESIS, is destroyed! There are many many ways The Bible and science teach the Earth with life, sin and death were here long BEFORE GENESIS! I will go into the details later, but for now I will simply point out that there was plenty of sin and death on Earth BEFORE GENESIS, when Adam sinned! The Devil was here full of deceit and malice "sin," before Adam sinned! In fact even Eve sinned before Adam! Yet it was Adam who brought sin and death into this-present-cosmos. So cosmos in Romans 5:12 can't mean the planet Earth.

FIVE

Occam's Razor

IN ORDER TO FIND TRUTHS IN OUR CREATIONISTS'/EVOLUTIONISTS' debates, it's essential that we rely on Occam's Razor. That basically means, "If they make sense, we must take the simplest-explanations over the more-complex, and base our beliefs on what we SEE and KNOW over what we assume, imagine and/or concoct." We must rely on facts rather than make up stories that back our beliefs. When a theory or hypothesis is lacking in evidence or requires wild-incoherent-absurdness, we must be willing to admit it's probably wrong. Due to Shermer's "believing-brain," this may be difficult. Let us pray, "Oh Lord, may reader and writer alike, keep an open-mind when reading Your two Books: The Book of Nature and The Bible. May we humbly learn before You when we ponder Your awesome-works! May we allow You to tell us what happened, without adding or subtracting from what You've told us in Your two Books."

In nature, my field of knowledge concerns bees and wasps. I wrote 34 articles about them (with photos), for The Poughkeepsie Journal. I relied on world-renowned authors and experts; Thomas D. Seeley (honey bees), John W. Wenzel and James M. Carpenter (yellowjackets), and the late Robbin W. Thorp (bumble bees). Through these entomologists I learned about the unthinkable-abilities these primitive-insects have! Each task is extremely-difficult, despite the fact that they easily-perform-them! And the wonder is, according to entomologists, they-cannot-reason. They wonderfully-coordinate-their-tasks in ways far beyond-astonishment! This is even true when there are billions of Argentine ants that have "worked together" to stretch their colony for 3,700 miles in Southern Europe. There can be 60,000 honey bees in a single ultra-complicated-colony! There are undertakers that remove the dead bees (preventing diseases), some bees build perfect hexagon cells to raise the brood in or store honey in (an extreme-wonder in itself), some feed the larvae, some feed the queen, some gather nectar, some collect pollen, some get water and when needed, some fan the nest with their wings to keep it from overheating and some guard the hive. At all times they all must know what to do and perform it! Any breakdown would kill the colony. I know one thing--Somebody reasoned! Are we seeing the mind-of-God or mindless-nature (natural selection)? What Job said is pertinent here, "Behold, these are but the fringes of His ways." (Job 26:14). A Psalmist said, "His understanding is infinite." (Psalm147:5). For an in-depth look into the wonder of honey bees, see Seeley's books. Additionally, these entomologists taught me that the dictionaries spell bumble bee, honey bee and yellowjacket wrong (see my: "Bumblebee or Bumble Bee"/Poughkeepsie Journal).

When it comes to yellowjackets, mysteries abound! Top entomologists who've spent their lives trying to discover how they know, for example, when it's time to build bigger cells for the large females, which when mated become "gynes," which when they have offspring, become "queens." (Honey bee queens, on the other hand, are born queens, since there are thousands of bees already there in her colony.) Many yellowjacket-mysteries, as far as anyone knows, are beyond knowing! I say this because the best minds in the field have been unable to solve them! In the classic, ("The Social Biology of Wasps" edited by Kenneth G. Ross and Robert W. Matthews p. 480), John W. Wenzel admits, "Naturalists have long been fascinated with the nests of social insects because their architectural complexity contrasts with the builders' presumably limited intelligence; the origin and significance of this complexity remain major unsolved problems in understanding the evolution of nest architecture." On page 508 Wenzel further admits, "Our understanding of the origin and function of various nest structures remains largely speculative, since stenogastrine biology is still poorly known ..." Albert Greene (p. 286), said, "Cell construction presents an additional suite of problems, including how uniformity is achieved in cell shape and what factors are responsible for cell initiation." "The mechanism by which worker cell size is gradually increased throughout the season and the basis for the quantum leap to reproductive cell construction are still unknown." By "reproductive," he's referring to the much larger queen cells. They must be made late in the season so the new queens can be alive when the time comes to hibernate. Everything is so precise! How they know when to make bigger queen cells, is a mystery known only to God! Greene further states on page 305, "The physiological mechanisms that stimulate queen production are unknown." "what is visible represents only the surface of their world." He concludes his study with a rhetorical question: "In view of the frustratingly tentative nature of this summary, how much is really known about yellowjackets?" Job spoke of God Who, "does awesome things that cannot be fathomed." (Job 5:9).

God has arranged it so I'm able to determine whether or not these insects could've lived through a global flood, which helps determine what must've happened BEFORE GENESIS and during Noah's Flood. And by the way, the knowledge the above entomologists have (or had--Robbin passed away), about these three insects (except how they got here-they're evolutionists), surpasses that of any creationist I've found. This is why, throughout, I emphasize: "Though evolutionists do not know how any animals got here, there's a lot we can learn from them. They're not wrong about most things! Hear them out concerning cosmology, geology, and biology. Admit it when their knowledge surpasses creationists in some areas. In science,there are far more evolutionists than creationists, so we'd be foolish to simply write-off all-of-their-knowledge!" Many of these evolutionists haven't been been shown good reasons to become creationists. To some extent Creationists are to blame! We must admit it when our knowledge, in some areas, is superficial compared to theirs. Don't throw out the baby with the bathwater! Even Jesus said, concerning at least one area of life, "for the sons of this world are in their generation wiser than the children of light." (Luke 16:8 KJV).

I do not believe any piece of literature has been analyzed as often or in such detail as Genesis chapter one. Especially the first two verses! They have been taken apart and turned inside-out! They have been analyzed, scrutinized, and synthesized like no other piece-of-literature! Every word has been carefully studied in detail to find its meaning! The Hebrew-grammar has been mulled-over by our top-scholars. Science has been called upon for help. Despite all of the research, to this day, there is no strong-consensus concerning what Genesis actually says. The best I can do is to humbly show you what I've come to believe and why, after casting-myself-upon-God for His mercy and help!

Though The Bible doesn't go into the details of science, it does tell us some of the basics. It gives God the credit and glory for creating everything that exists. Did The Bible's purposeful-God; having infinite-brilliance, power and skill, create everything or not? Did the songs of birds, the colors and designs of butterfly wings, the hexagon-building and honey-making abilities of honey bees and the brilliant-brains of evolutionists, who are able to make the impossible seem plausible or probable (or even certain), arise from The Bible's God or from a-mindless-primeval-soup? The Bible's writers were serious, highly-educated, no-nonsense, clear-thinking people who did not tolerate illogical-ideas.

Moses was probably the wisest and most knowledgeable-man-on-Earth, combining face-to-face conversations (Exodus chapters 19-34) with God with being, "educated in all the wisdom of Egypt" (Acts 7:22). He was uniquely-qualified to write Genesis. At the time of Exodus, only Moses could go close to God and when he came down from Mount Sanai, "his face shown because of his speaking with Him." (Exodus 34:29).

The Apostle Paul, the most-prolific-New-Testament-writer, was taught by the famed Rabbi, Gamaliel (Acts 5:33-39, 22:3). Indeed when he (in chains for preaching the Gospel), was before King Festus, he spoke of how when he persecuted Christians, Christ's light knocked him and his companions off their feet and blinded him. Festus said, "Paul, you are beside yourself; much learning has driven you mad." (Acts 26:24).

The Apostle Peter might have been a fisherman, but he had a-logical-and-quick-mind that connected-facts-wonderfully, and was an articulate-orator with a great-memory (see his awesome-message in Acts 3:12-26).

The Apostle John's Gospel required that he, as all Bible-authors, be a special-person, prepared-by-God. Dionysius, Bishop of Alexandria (AD 262), points out that there are no language-errors in the Gospel or Epistle of John which were written, "with the greatest elegance, both in their expressions and in their reasoning, and in the whole structure of their style. For, as might be presumed, the writer possessed the gift of both kinds of discourse, the Lord having bestowed both these capacities upon him--that of knowledge and of expression."

The prophet Daniel was able to understand mysteries better than anyone in the world. Daniel 1:4 shows he already had every kind of wisdom, understanding and knowledge when he was taught in the literature-and-language-of-the-Chaldeans. He was "ten times better than all of the magicians and conjurers in Nebuchadnezzar's kingdom." (Dan.1:20). Note that, "MOSES HAVING BEEN TAUGHT BY EGYPTIANS AND DANIEL BY CHALDEEANS, SHOWS GOD IS NOT AGAINST US LEARNING FROM NON-BIBLE-BELIEVING PEOPLE." History confirms, "Daniel was made co-ruler over all of Babylon" (Dan. 5:29). When God through Ezekiel, wanted to show the King of Tyre how out-of-control his pride was, He said,

"In your-proud-heart ... you think you're wiser than Daniel." (Ezekiel 28:3). Though Daniel lived over 2,500 years ago, some of his end-time prophecies have recently come true (i.e. "Men will zoom back and forth and knowledge will multiply" Dan. 12:4), with the rest soon to follow. His prophecies concerning Babylon, Medo-Persia, Greece and Rome (Dan. 11:5-35), came true in the fourth to second centuries B. C., baffling skeptics.

Though these Prophets and Apostles were gifted, they did not rely on their own abilities. They did not have high opinions of themselves. The Apostle Paul said, "Not that we are adequate in ourselves to consider anything as from ourselves, but our adequacy is from God." (II Corinthians 3:5).

Paul also said, "Let no man deceive himself. If any man among you thinks that he is wise in this age, he must become foolish in his own eyes, so that he may become wise. For the wisdom of this cosmos is foolishness before God. For it is written, 'He is the One Who catches the wise in their own craftiness.' and again, 'The Lord knows the reasonings of the wise, that they are useless and empty.'" (1 Cor. 3:18, 19).

The Bible, being the Word of God, beat modern science to the basics by 1,900 to 3,600 years in the following ways.

1. In Hebrews 11:3, the Apostle Paul said, "what is seen was not made out of things which are visible." We now know that everything we see is made out of invisible-atoms.
2. In Isaiah 44:24, God said, "I, Yahweh, Am the maker of all things, spreading out the heavens by Myself." We have recently confirmed that the heavens are spreading out--and we don't understand why the process is speeding up.
3. In Job 38: 4,5; God tells Job that the size of the Earth was determined by Him. Solomon put it this way, "The Lord used wisdom in creating the Earth." (Proverbs 3: 19). We now know that if the Earth was much-smaller-or-bigger, life could not exist here.

4. We recently learned that the Earth, sun, moon and stars have not always existed. At some point there was a beginning. The Apostle John said, "In the beginning was the Word and the Word was with God and the Word was God. He was in the beginning with God. All things came into being through Him and apart from Him nothing came into being that has come into being." "And the Word became flesh and dwelt among us ..." (John 1:1-3, 14).

5. Ezekiel chapter 10, thousands of years before the Wright brothers, showed that technology to make flying machines, was possible.

6. The top experts in the modern world, including David M. Jacobs, are telling us that an alarming number of women, world-wide, are producing hybrids after being impregnated by strange humanoids aboard UFOs. The story is the same everywhere. The Bible predicts this weirdness would be going on in these last days. Jesus said that when He returns it will be, "just as it happened in the days of Noah" (Luke 17:26). Before Noah's flood, "The Nephilim were on the earth in those days and also afterward, when the sons of God came into the daughters of men." (Genesis 6:4). To be "the sons of God," here refers to beings created directly by God (i. e. Angels, who in this case have fallen). In the oldest book in The Bible, "the sons of God," are obviously angels (Job 38:7). This kind of thing has probably usually gone on, but peaked in the days of Noah and is peaking now. But how does The Bible indicate that this takes place aboard UFOs? It's the Apostle Paul who puts the finishing touches on this Biblical prediction when he speaks of: "spiritual wickedness in the heavens." (Ephesians 6:12). Somehow, the great Biblical genius/Bible-scholar, Watchman Nee, knew this strange mating was going on before the 1950s.

7. "When Elizabeth heard Mary's (pregnant with Jesus), greeting, the baby (John The Baptist) leaped in her womb." (Luke 1:41).

Just because babies are in the womb, doesn't mean they're not babies with the ability to learn, know, remember and have-intuition. We now know babies can remember music they heard four months before birth. We know they dream and can clap their hands long-before-birth. When P. M. H. Atwater (L. H. D.), traveled the country researching near death experiences in children, several mothers who contemplated aborting their children, volunteered the following: "When my child was old enough to confront me, he/she asked, 'Why did you think about killing me when I was inside you?'" (Coast To Coast AM (radio), circa 2000).

In the January/February 2011 issue of Discover Magazine, # 75 of the top 100 stories of 2010, is titled: "Social Life Begins in the Womb." This study showed that fetal twins between 14 and 18 weeks of gestation, "recognized and responded to the other twin." They treated each other gently, whereas they forcibly kicked and shoved the uterine wall.

In 1981 French geneticist Jerome L. LeJeune told a United States-Senate-subcommittee: "To accept the fact that after fertilization has taken place a new human has come into being is no longer a matter of taste or opinion. The human nature of the human being, from conception to old age, is not a metaphysical contention; it is plain experimental evidence."

Thanks to a highly-sophisticated-Stanford-machine, it is now known that the real you--your-personality, your-consciousness, your-mind, your-soul; resides-in-your-heart. Your heart sends thoughts to your head. Something in your heart thinks first! When an idea is sent from your heart, strange-to-say, it's never-wrong! And scientists were astonished to discover that the heart knows what will happen a few seconds before it happens! And the voice is never wrong! This Stanford study has been confirmed by other studies around the world. Nikola Tesla said, "But instinct is something which transcends knowledge.

We have, undoubtedly, certain finer fibers that enable us to perceive truths when logical deduction, or any other willful effort of the brain, is futile." "My brain is only a receiver, in the Universe there is a core from which we obtain knowledge, strength and inspiration." He also said, "The scientists of today think deeply instead of clearly. One must be sane to think clearly, but one can think deeply and be quite insane."

Another fact that should be noted, is that when people get a heart-transplant, they more or less become like the person that donated it.. People with no-musical-abilities become proficient-in-music when they receive the heart-of-a-musician!

Jeremiah said, "Now the word of Yahweh came to me saying, 'Before I formed you in the womb, I knew you.'" (jer. 1:4-5).

In F. W. Grant's commentary in his NUMERICAL BIBLE (1903), he said, "what then, is this name 'Yahweh?" Almost the whole consensus of commentators agree and I see no possible ground of dissent from it, that it means HE WHO IS. Thus the connection with 'I AM,' which Lord's words to Moses naturally imply, is clear at once."

Most important of all, God can make Himself known intuitively when we listen to His Word being preached. Only prayer can open our hearts to "know God." I don't know how prayer works, but I know it does!

Concerning little-babies-and-abortion, we do not need new-laws as much as new-hearts. Abortionists need more than changed-minds--they need changed-hearts! They must be changed in their-deepest-beings!

8. We now know that even the simplest form of life is so extremely complex that we can apply Romans 1:20 to it, "For since the creation of the world, His invisible attributes, His eternal power and divine nature, have been clearly seen, being understood through what has been made, so that they are without excuse." With today's powerful telescopes and microscopes, there's less excuse than ever.

SIX

The Entertaining Creation/Evolution Debate

I DON'T SUPPOSE THERE'S ANY OTHER DEBATE WHERE FACTS ARE hidden, distorted and neglected as they are in this one. People who believe-in-impossibilities are sure they're right. Relatively-few are aware of the main-theories-and-arguments. There are those who think if they say something loud-enough and often-enough, they will persuade-themselves-and-others. For many it's very difficult or nearly impossible to be open-minded to new-concepts concerning the history of animal life. This debate is so strange that we have evolutionists who admit they don't see any way it could've happened and creationists who insist that it did!?!? With so many different things being said, it's not easy to sort it all out. There's a huge amount of dishonesty! The debate often gets extremely heated. Some of you think the Earth and Universe were created in six days a few thousand years ago. Others think Earth is over 4 billion and the Universe is over 13 billion. Some of you think life came about through and evolved by natural processes. Others think God created everything. Since I'm talking to all of you here, at times what I say will not be directly aimed at you. At times I'll be talking to you who believe the Earth and Universe are billions of years old, and at other times to you who think they were created in Six Days a few thousand years ago. Hopefully it will be interesting and educational to see other viewpoints! I hope to make this study of extremely contentious issues as much fun as possible. And I admit, that won't be easy! My hope is that *facts* will win the day!

Creationist beliefs have been all over the map! According to Ronald L. Numbers a few months after the highly-influential book, "The Genesis Flood" appeared, Whitcomb wrote to Morris, "As you know I have been somewhat embarrassed about the situation, since practically everyone I know takes the gap theory or the day-age theory, even though they seem to be happy about our position on the flood!" ("The Creationists" p. 230). New facts have changed Gappers and Day-Agers minds, and now they are not happy with the Global Noah's Flood position. Neither the Gap nor the Day-Age dominate as they once did because, the rather new singular dominate position is, Young Earth Creationism (YEC). Unfortunately there's a great deal of un-Christian-hostility involved that surfaces in this debate! On page 232 of "The Scandal of the Evangelical Mind," (Christianity Today's 1994 Book of the Year), Mark A. Noll said, "The modern evangelical church is extremely sensitive about open discussion of scientific issues that bear on Genesis 1-11. Enough Christians are so afraid of what might turn up in such discussions that anyone who does try to explore the issues is in ecclesiastical jeopardy." We must take to heart what Noll says on pages 202-203, "Now, it is a disgraceful and dangerous thing for an infidel to hear a Christian, presumably giving the meaning of Holy Scripture, talking nonsense on these topics; and we should take all means to prevent such an embarrassing situation, in which people show up vast ignorance in a Christian and laugh it to scorn. The shame is not so much that an ignorant individual is derided, but that people outside the household of faith think our sacred writers held such opinions, and, to the great loss of those for whose salvation we toil, the writers of our Scripture are criticized and rejected as unlearned men."

Evolutionists argue with one another over things like whether evolution is always a slow gradual Darwin-type-process, or at times it can happen at an accelerated speed and whether there's a God or not. Creationists argue over things like the age of the universe, what happened in Genesis One, the severity and scope of Noah's Flood and the length of the Seven Days of the Creation week. The main event pits evolutionists against creationists. The most important determination concerns whether The Bible's infinitely intelligent, powerful, purposeful and skillful God created the Universe and all animals basically as they are or did purposeless random processes do it?

A large portion of the scientific community does not seek truth. They're goal is to rid the world of The Bible's God. My 50+years of research tells me many who become scientists, do so to prove there's no need for a God. It's a form of escapism! They are terrified of The Bible's Holy, sin-hating God! In the final-analysis, "The reason so many scientists are atheists is because, THEY HATE GOD! So how do you reach people who close their eyes to the truth? It's a daunting task,impossible without deep prayer. The Apostle Paul said of those who "would not believe" (Acts 28:24), "they have closed their eyes" (Acts 28:27). But of course there are many scientists with open-minds, shown by the fact that hundreds of creationist books are written by former evolutionists. Modern scientific facts are turning scientists away from evolution and toward creationism, instead of the other way around.

We creationists are in hostile territory. We are in a world-system that hates God with an all-consuming passion! That's the reason we have the absurdness of atheism! That's the reason atheists want to outlaw Christianity and put an end to the discussion and make owning a Bible against the law, like in places such as China. That's the reason there's an irrational hate of the Jews! That's the reason we have the term, "antisemitism." Antisemitism is a well-known, widespread phenomenon and I don't recall "anti" any other nationality held in such a widespread way! And why does this insanity exist? Simply because Satan hates the Jews intensely and spreads that hate in the hearts of many of his followers. That's why the Apostle Paul called the devil, "the spirit that is now working in the sons of disobedience" (Ephesians 2:2). That also explains why The Bible, out of all books, is so hated and banned. The devil doesn't want you to read it!

It may seem strange beyond comprehension, but Jesus (the eternal Son) became a Jew and therefore, "Salvation is from the Jews." (John 4:22).

SEVEN

Does Life Require The Bible's Awesome God?
(Refuting The All-Time Greatest Myth Of Them All)

IN "A PHYSICIST LOOKS AT EVOLUTION," PHYSICS BULLETIN, VOL. 31 (May 1980), p. 31, H. S. Lipson said, "If living matter is not then, caused by the interplay of atoms, natural forces and radiation, how has it come into being? ... I think, however, that we must ... admit that the only acceptable explanation is creation. I know that this is anathema to physicists, as indeed it is to me, but we must not reject a theory that we do not like if the experimental evidence supports it." It has been my experience that words like these, far too often, fall on deaf ears. These evolutionists are an example of the people spoken of by The Apostle Paul, "For the time will come when they will not endure sound doctrine; but wanting to have their ears tickled, they will accumulate for themselves teachers in accordance with their own desires, and will turn their ears away from the truth and will turn aside to myths." (II Timothy 4: 3,4). Of course, the greatest myth, as we'll now see, is that life could exist without God creating it.

Dr. George Wald, 1971 Professor Emeritus of biology at Harvard (1971 Nobel Prize winner in biology), said, "There are only two possibilities as to how life arose. One is spontaneous generation arising to evolution. The other is a supernatural creative act of God. Spontaneous generation: that life arose from non-living matter was scientifically disproved 120 years ago by Louis Pasteur and others.

That leaves us with only one possible conclusion, that life arose from a supernatural creative act of God. I will not accept that because I do not want to believe in God. Therefore I choose to believe in that which I know is scientifically impossible: that life arose spontaneously from non-living matter." (Wald, George, "Innovation and Biology," Scientific American, Vol. 199, Sept. 1958, p. 100)

When Jun-Yuan Chen, the head paleontologist at Chengjiang, wove some criticism of Darwinism into his lectures here, he asked why he got a cool response. He was told, "Criticizing Darwinian theory is unpopular in the United States." He laughed and famously said, "In China we can criticize Darwin, but not the government; in America, you can criticize the government, but not Darwin."

John Horgan said, "In short, proteins cannot form without DNA, but neither can DNA form without proteins." ("In The Beginning," Scientific American, February 1991, p. 120).

Francis Crick, (co-founder of DNA), Sir Fred Hoyle (former University Lecturer in Mathematics at Cambridge University) and Chandra Wickramasinghe (former Professor of Applied Math & Astronomy, University College, Cardiff) threw a huge monkey wrench into all evolutionary concepts concerning how life began.

We will begin by seeing how Crick and Hoyle used math to destroy the long-held evolutionary belief that life started on Earth without the aid of an intelligent God. This will be followed by Wickramasinghe joining them to prove that life could not have begun anywhere in the Universe without a super-intellect.

Frances Crick said, "This is an easy exercise in combinatorials. Suppose the chain is about two hundred amino acids long; this is, if anything rather less than the average length of proteins of all types. Since we have just twenty possibilities at each place, the number of possibilities is twenty multiplied by itself some two hundred times. This is conveniently written 20 to the power 200 and is approximately equal to 10 to the power of 260, that is a one followed by 260 zeros. ... Moreover, we have only considered a polypeptide chain of rather modest length. Had we considered longer ones as well, the figure would have been even more immense … The great majority of sequences can never have been synthesized at all, at any time."

"An honest man, armed with all the knowledge available to us now, could only state that in some sense, the origin of life appears at the moment to be almost a miracle, so many are the conditions which would have had to have been satisfied to get it going." ("Life Itself: It's Origin and Nature" pp. 51-2, 88)

In the "New Scientist," Vol. 92 (Nov. 19, 1981), pp. 526-7, Sir Fred Hoyle said, "I don't know how long it is going to be before astronomers generally recognize that the combinatorial arrangement of not even one among many thousands of biopolymers on which life depends could have been arrived at by natural processes here on the earth. Astronomers will have a little difficulty at understanding this because they will be assured by biologists that it is not so, the biologists having been assured in their turn by others that it is not so. The others are a group of persons who believe, quite openly, in mathematical miracles. They advocate the belief that tucked away in nature, outside of normal physics, there is a law which performs miracles (provided the miracles are in the aid of biology). This curious situation sits oddly on a profession that for long has been dedicated to coming up with logical explanations of biblical miracles. … It is quite otherwise, however, with the modern mathematical miracle workers, who are always found to be living in the twilight fringes of thermodynamics."

"At all events, anyone with even a nodding acquaintance with the Rubic cube will concede the near-impossibility of a solution being obtained by a blind person moving the cubic faces at random. Now imagine 10 to the power of 50 blind persons each with a scrambled Rubic cube, and try to conceive of the chance of them all simultaneously arriving at the solved form. You then have the chance of arriving by random shuffling of just one of the many biopolymers on which life depends. The notion that not only the biopolymers but the operating programme of a living cell could be arrived at by chance in a primordial soup here on the Earth is evidently nonsense of a high order. Life must plainly be a cosmic phenomenon."

Sir Fred Hoyle and Chandra Wickramasinghe, "Evolution from Space" (1984-- p. 148); "No matter how large the environment one considers, life cannot have had a random beginning. Troops of monkeys thundering away at random on typewriters could not produce the works of Shakespeare, for the practical reason that the whole observable universe is not large enough to contain the necessary monkey hordes, the necessary typewriters and certainly not the waste paper baskets required for the deposition of wrong attempts. The same is true for living material."

"The likelihood of the spontaneous formation of life from inanimate matter is one to a number with 40,000 noughts after it … It is big enough to bury Darwin and the whole theory of evolution. There was no primeval soup, neither on this planet nor on any other, and if the beginnings of life were not random, they must therefore have been the product of purposeful intelligence."

Hoyle, Sir Fred, "The Intelligent Universe" (1983--pp. 20-21) "If there were a basic principle of matter which somehow drove organic systems toward life, its existence should easily be demonstrated in the laboratory. One could, for instance, take a swimming bath to represent the primordial soup. Fill it with any chemicals you please, and shine any kind of radiation on it that takes your fancy. Let the experiment proceed for a year and see how many of those 2,000 enzymes [proteins produced by living cells] have appeared in the bath. I will give the answer, and so save the time and trouble and expense of actually doing the experiment. You would find nothing at all, except possibly for a tarry sludge composed of amino acids and other simple organic chemicals. How can I be so confident of this statement? Well, if it were otherwise, the experiment would long since been done and would be well-known and famous throughout the world. The cost of it would be trivial compared to the cost of landing a man on the Moon."

Chandra Wickramasinghe, in an interview in the "London Daily

Express," (August 14, 1981), said, "From my earliest training as a scientist, I was very strongly brainwashed to believe that science cannot be consistent with any kind of deliberate creation. That notion has had to be painfully shed." "They did the calculations based on the size and age of the universe (15 billion years) and found that the odds against life beginning spontaneously anywhere in space were '10 to the power of 30.'"

The magazine, "The Good News," Jan./Feb. 2006, says, "Recently, one of the world's most renowned atheists, Sir Anthony Flew, renounced his atheism because of the compelling evidence of the DNA molecule." Flew said, "It now seems to me that the findings of more than fifty years of DNA research have provided materials for a new and enormously powerful argument for design ... Biologists' investigation of DNA has shown, by the almost unbelievable complexity of the arrangements which are needed to produce (life), that intelligence must have been involved." He "Had to go where the evidence leads." (Famous Atheist Now Believes in God, Dec. 9, 2004, A. P. report)

In "Darwin On Trial" p. 105, Phillip E. Johnson said, "Although some components of living systems can be duplicated with very advanced techniques, scientists employing the full power of their intelligence cannot manufacture living organisms from amino acids, sugars, and the like. How then was the trick done before scientific intelligence was in existence? The simplest organism capable of independent life, the prokaryote bacterial cell, is a masterpiece of miniaturized complexity which makes a spaceship seem rather low-tech."

In Genesis 18:14 God "Yahweh" (He Who Is), asked Abraham, "Is anything too difficult for God?" Evolutionists ask, "Is anything too difficult for nothing?" In Psalm 139:12 Solomon's father, King David, said, "Even the darkness is not dark to You, and the night is as bright as the day."

Famed Reformed radio/television minister, R. C. Sproul has pointed out that, "Chance is really nothing. It exerts no power at all.

A coin may end up heads or tails by chance, but chance does not help flip the coin. So if you start with nothing and work on it with nothing, you end up with everything! That's evolution!" R. C. said when he told an evolutionist this, "The man hit himself in the middle of his forehead with the palm of his hand and said, 'Of course!'"

World-famous astrophysicist, Michio Kaku, said, "I have concluded that we are in a world made by rules created by an intelligence. For me it is clear that we exist in a plan which is governed by rules that were created, shaped by a universal intelligence and not by chance."

THE BAFFLING TWO-SPOTTED
FIELD CRICKET EMBRYOS

Harvard geneticist, Dr. Cassandra Extavour, wondered: "How do embryo cells--cells that have the same genome but aren't doing the same thing with that information--know where to go and what to do?" She said, "Some other mechanism was at work in the cricket embryo. The researchers spent hours watching and analizing the microscopic dance of nuclei: glowing nubs dividing and moving in a puzzling pattern, not altogether orderly, not quite random, at varying directions and speeds, neighboring nuclei more in sync than those farther away. The performance suggested a choreography beyond mere physics or chemistry. information--know where to go and what to do?" No wonder Job speaks of "God; Who does great and unsearchable things, wonders without number." (Job 5:9). This is only a tiny portion of "The wonders of One perfect in knowledge." (Job 37:16).

DID GOD CREATE ALL PLANTS AND
ANIMALS FULLY-FORMED?

The Bible tells us God made animals fully-formed without having to evolve (Genesis 1:20-25). Evolutionists say, "All animals' ancestry can be traced back to a the simplest possible life-form." They believe in "mold-to-man!" I believe all animals were made in a way similar to how Adam was: "Then God 'Yahweh' (He Who Is) formed man from dust of the ground and breathed into his nostrils the breath of life; and man became a living soul." (Gen. 2:7). So which is right? How is it that there are elephants, ants, elk and antelopes; honey badgers, honey suckles, honey locusts and honey bees; humming birds, horses, hornets and humans; and bats, beetles, butterflies and buffalo? Did God originally make the plants and animals basically as they are now or did they evolve completely new body plans and abilities, starting from a primeval soup? Have scientists finally learned the truth behind what The Bible told us long ago? Let's find out!

In 1988, after searching for evidence of evolution for forty years, Nils Herbert-Nilsson wrote, "The fossil material is now so complete that it has been possible to construct new classes, and the lack of transitional series cannot be explained as being due to the scarcity of material. The deficiencies are real; they will never be filled ... The idea of an evolution rests on pure belief."

The late, Dr. Colin Patterson, former senior paleontologist (fossil expert) at the British Museum of Natural History, speaking at the monthly meeting of the "Systematics Discussion Group," in the NYC Museum of Natural History on November 5, 1981, said: " ...I'm speaking on two subjects, evolutionism and creationism, and I believe it's true to say that I know nothing whatever about either ... One of the reasons I started taking this anti-evolutionary view, well, let's call it non-evolutionary, was last year I had a sudden realization. One morning I woke up..and it struck me that I had been working on this stuff for twenty years, and there was not one thing I knew about it." He added: "That was quite a shock that one could be misled for so long." During a public lecture, Patterson asked the geology staff in the Field Museum of Natural History in Chicago, "Can you tell me anything you know about evolution, any one thing that you think is true?" All he got was silence! He said, "I tried it on the members of the Evolutionary

Morphology Seminar in the University of Chicago..and all I got there was silence for a long time, and then eventually one person said: 'Yes, I do know one thing. It ought not to be taught in high school.'"

Nobody has seen a chain of animals in the process making a new species! Not Moses! Not Solomon! Not Socrates! Not Josephus! Not Plato! Not Herodotus! Not Jesus! Not the Apostles! Not any scientist! And not me!

THE GENESIS ONE MYSTERY: WHY THE DEBATE RAGES

Why hasn't a Genesis One belief-system gained a consensus in our time? How is it no Bible scholar or group of Bible scholars has been able to explain what Moses wrote in a way that would persuade most Christians? The state of this matter means, at the very least, most Christians are clinging to an incorrect Genesis One interpretation. With all of the modern scholarship being easily accessible on the internet, it doesn't seem possible no conclusion has a consensus.

There are many who fiercely defend a position without knowing what the implications are. They are unaware of the problems that need to be solved. Nobody has ever shown them the weaknesses of their beliefs.

How can it be that in the last 150 years, there have been major shifts in what the majority of Bible scholars, and therefore most Christians, have believed? How can it be that it's about an even split between those who think the Bible teaches the Universe was made in six days a few thousand years ago and those who believe science and The Bible combine to teach it's billions of years old.. This means that at least about half the Christian-world is wrong! Is everyone reading the same Bible? Bernard Ramm, said, "The gap theory has become the standard interpretation throughout hyper-orthodoxy, appearing in an endless stream of books, booklets, Bible studies, and periodical articles. In fact, it has become so sacrosanct with some, that to question it is equivalent to tampering with Sacred Scripture or to manifest modernistic leanings." ("The Christian View of Science and Scripture" 1954, p. 135). The Gap Theory, due to modern scholarship, has since fallen out of favor. For decades I was a "Gapper," but when it was proven untenable, I was forced to move on. Some of the main creationist theories have been totally disproved and many huge problems have arisen among the rest. As of today, the scholars in each camp have pointed out seemingly insurmountable troubling-facts found in rival-camps. If a major point in a belief-system has been shown to be wrong, its scenario cannot stand. Of course, this means that right now out of those proposing one of the most-believed theories, hardly anybody and maybe nobody, is right. That's the mystery that confronts us at the moment. How much do those who are teaching us, really know about Genesis One?

THE SIX DAYS OF GENESIS

So exactly what happened during the Six Days? I will explain why I think they were merely about restoration/revealing/arraying/repairing of a recently judged local portion of land (the Mesopotamian-area). Hereafter I will use (YEC) for Young Earth Creationists or Creationism and (AEC) for Ancient Earth Creationists or Creationism. One of the main Biblical points I'll be making related to Biblical creationism is that, as the small sampling of **scholars** below (a virtual who's who in the recent Christian world), believe or believed (in the case of those who have passed away), **Earth had a long history, with Lucifer as its king, prophet and high priest BEFORE GENESIS! They are: Watchman Nee, Donald Grey Barnhouse, F. W, Grant, Merrill F. Unger, Allen P. Ross, F. F. Bruce, Jack Van Impe, C. I. Scofield, Derek Prince, Billy Graham, Jay Vernon McGee, R. A, Torrey, G. H, Pember and Finis Jennings Drake.**

I realize much of what I say will be new to many of you. I'm just asking you to be open-minded and **consider the facts.** Don't be like Eliphaz, one of Job's "comforters," who dogmatically supposed that what he had always believed (that extreme suffering always came because of sin) must be correct! Not knowing that God was praising Job and showing him off to Satan (Job 1:8), Eliphaz told Job, "Remember now, who ever perished being innocent? Or where were the upright destroyed? According to what I have seen, those who plow iniquity and those who sow trouble, harvest it," (4:7-8). We shouldn't be so sure of ourselves! Eliphaz, though way-off, was certain he was right! Creationism is important, but our belief here is not a basis for fellowship. We must love one another regardless of whether we see-eye-to-eye or not! There's no need to be militant. Tolerance of others' alternative-beliefs is essential to "walk in a manner worthy of the calling with which you have been called, with all humility and gentleness, with patience, showing tolerance for one another in love, being diligent to preserve the unity of the Spirit in the bond of peace." (Ephesians 4:1-3).

EIGHT

We Must Humbly Admit We May Be Wrong

JAMES 3:2 SAYS, "FOR WE ALL STUMBLE IN MANY WAYS." THE BIBLE has many examples of people who stumbled in their opinions, including of themselves! This leads to trusting in self, rather than in God for strength and knowledge. Stephen Hawking said, "Religion: a fairy tale for people afraid of the dark." John Lennox said, "Atheism: a fairy tale for people afraid of the light." We all need God's light in many ways! Otherwise we remain in deep spiritual darkness! The first words spoken in the Bible, were God's, "Let there be light!" Isaiah 2:5 says, "Come, let us walk in the light of Yahweh." David said, "In Your light we see light." (Psalm 36:9). Matthew 4:16 says, "The people who were sitting in darkness saw a great light," Jesus told the crowds of His followers, "You are the light of the world. A city set on a hill cannot be hidden; nor does anyone light a lamp and put it under a basket, but on a lampstand, and it gives light to all who are in the house. Let your light shine before men in such a way that they may see your good works, and glorify your Father who is in heaven." (Matt. 5:14-16). We must determine if there are baskets in our lives covering the light of Christ within us? Jesus is the light "I Am the light of the world." (John 8:12), but His words were also full of the light of instruction! Right here is the greatest problem! "This is the judgment, that light has come into the world, and men loved the darkness rather than the Light, for their deeds were evil." (John 3:19). Let's search for His Light!

"At that time the disciples came to Jesus and said, 'Who is greatest in the kingdom of heaven?' And He called a child to Him and set him before them, and said, 'Truly I say to you, unless you are converted and become like children, you will not enter the kingdom of heaven. Whoever then humbles himself as this child, he is the greatest in the kingdom of heaven.'" (Matt. 18:1-4). These disciples, including Peter (Matt. 16:15-17), were already born-again-Christians! The question was: "Will they attain greatness in God's eyes?" A little later in Mark 14:27-29, we find the following: "And Jesus said to them, "You will all fall away, because it is written, 'I will strike down the Shepherd, and the sheep shall be scattered.' 'But after I have been raised, I will go ahead of you into Galilee.' But Peter said to Him, 'Though all may fall away, yet I will not!'" In 14:66-72, we have the account of Peter before a servant-girl, denying that he knew Jesus! When he realized his cowardice in denying his Lord, "he began to weep bitterly." I don't believe God could use Peter, until he considered everyone better than himself! The Apostle Paul called himself: "chief of all sinners," and "the very least of all saints." (I Timothy 1:15, Ephesians 3:8). Jesus said, "I Am the Light of the world." "Those who sat in darkness saw a great light." "In Your light we see light."

NINE

Local Creationism And The Statement Of Fact View
(The Reasons I Believe Genesis One Is Only About A Local Area)

I'M PROBABLY THE ONLY PERSON ON EARTH WHO THINKS GENESIS One is only about a local creation (revealing/fixing/arraying). But I'm not the first! Dr. Terry Mortenson of AIG, said, "...in the late 1830s the evangelical Congregationalist theologian, John Pye-Smith (1774-1851), advocated a local creation and a local Flood, both of which occurred in Mesopotamia." (The Great Turning Point, p. 35). In "Sketch of the literary Life of Dr. John Pye-Smith, F. R. S. Smith, op. Cit., pp. Liii-liv.," John Hamilton Davies said, "Relying on EVIDENCE, the only valuable ally in science investigation, our author arrived at the conclusion ... that the Noachian deluge was not, and could not have been, universal and that the affirmation could not be maintained, except by the wretched subterfuge of supposing a stupendous miracle throughout the whole continuance of the Deluge." Pye-Smith realized, if Noah's Flood was local, then for the same geological-reasons, the Genesis 1:2 flood was local. After all, Archbishop James Ussher (1581-1656), only had 1,656 years between the two floods. ("The Annals of the World" p. 19). And even if we triple that, the geology would be the same. So there's been at least two Local Creationists! Thanks to tireless scholarly-research and accumulated-knowledge, the Hebrew Scriptures are better understood now, than at any time in church-history. Hugh Ross said, "Theologians and Bible scholars have rightfully argued that due to ongoing biblical scholarship former understandings of a particular text, such as one or more of the early chapters of Genesis, may need revision." (Navigating Genesis p. 21-22). I think, once seen, Local-Creationism may become widely-accepted! So let's have a look!

> 1. GOD DOES NOT SPEAK IN THE GENESIS 1:1,2 BEGINNING. "In the beginning God revealed/fixed/arrayed the local atmosphere and land, when the land was hidden and useless, and darkness was over the surface of the deep, and the Spirit of God was hovering over the surface of the waters." (Gen. 1:1,2, my literal translation). It would've been easy for Moses to have said, "In the beginning God said," but he didn't. When the very beginning is spoken of in John 1:1-3, the "Word" was there. God spoke at the beginning of the other five creation days 2-6, so if 1:1 was part of Day One, certainly Moses would've written that God spoke there too, instead of having Him speak for the first time in 1:3 when Day One began. The reason Moses doesn't have God speaking in 1:1 is because, it's only a statement of fact concerning two things God did during the Six Days when God did speak, and not an account of the action of God working. There's always a purpose concerning everything that's said or not said in The Bible. My calling 1:1 "a statement of fact," concerning two things God did during the Six Days (the revealing/fixing/arraying the local heavens and land-area), is a slight adjustment from modern scholars who call it: "a summary statement," concerning what God did during the Six Days, over the globe. This "summary statement" view is seen in Young's Literal Translation of 1:1-3, "In the beginning of God's preparing the heavens and the earth--the earth hath existed waste and void, and darkness [is] on the face of the deep, and the Spirit of God fluttering on

the face of the waters, and God saith, 'Let light be;' and light is." The NSRV says, "When God began to create the heavens and the earth, the earth was complete chaos" (1;1-2a). The reason I go with "statement of fact," rather than, "summary statement," is because 1:1 only concerns itself with two things (the local heavens and land area), and doesn't include animals, including Adam; and other information, which a "summary statement" logically would. Though we may say He "arrayed" it with plants (1:11-12). It is but a small step to go from the often cited, "summary statement" to "statement of fact."

2. THE HEBREW WORD (REESHECTH) TRANSLATED, "BEGINNING" DOES NOT NECESSARILY MEAN: "THE VERY BEGINNING." This is important because, if it did, it couldn't refer only to a local area of land. Psalm 111:10 speaks of the "beginning" (reeshecth) of wisdom. Jeremiah spoke of the "beginning" (reeshecth) of Zedekiah's reign (Jer. 28:1). Neither refers to the very beginning. One thing said of Merrill F. Unger, arguably the best Old Testament Bible scholar ever, "Unger had a talent for getting to the heart of a verse and its poignant meaning." (Introduction, Unger's Commentary on the Old Testament). He said, "'In the beginning.' These opening words of divine revelation have been almost universally assumed to describe the original creation of the earth and the universe in eternity past, as in John 1:3 and Colossians 1:16-17. But there are cogent reasons to believe a relative rather than an absolute beginning is envisioned. This view sets God's creative activity of the earth in a much later geological period in the preparation for the latecomer, man." (p.5). It is only a small step to say the same thing about a local-land-area!

3. THE HEBREW WORD "BAHRAH," WHICH I TRANSLATE, "REVEALED/FIXED/ARRAYED," DOES

NOT MEAN, "CREATE OUT OF NOTHING," NOR DOES IT EVER MEAN THAT IN THE OTHER PLACES IT'S USED IN THE OLD TESTAMENT. IN FACT, IT IS USED INTERCHANGABLY WITH "ASA" (TO WORK ON SOMETHING ALREADY THERE). In The Bible, God alone is said to "bahrah" something. But to call 1:1 "the original creation out of nothing," is based on a false assumption and not on knowledge. There's no OT word for "create out of nothing." It's not something Moses was concerned with. It's not a concept he spoke of.

4. "ALL THINGS" ARE NOT MENTIONED IN GENESIS 1:1, AND THE SIX DAYS ARE NOT MENTIONED IN THE JOHN 1:1-3 BEGINNING, WHERE "ALL THINGS" ARE CREATED. To the tens of millions of you who think Genesis 1:1 is the first part of Day One, I say, "Consider carefully this point and the first three above." When John speaks of the beginning of "all things," he doesn't say, "as Moses said." Furthermore, the Six Days aren't in Colossians 1:16-17 where it says: "For by Him ALL THINGS were created, in the heavens and on earth, visible and invisible, whether thrones or dominions or rulers or authorities--all things have been created through Him and for Him. He is before all things, and through Him all things hold together." No "thrones or dominions or rulers or authorities" were created in Genesis One, although they were certainly already there, since as we'll see later, Lucifer had ruled the Earth in ancient times, long before Genesis. Bruce K. Waltke started the rumor that "the heavens and the earth (land)," are a compound word in Hebrew, like "dragonfly," and refers to "everything." Now this, though untrue, is seen in many creationists' writings. In the very next verse, land (ertz) is separated from the heavens (shaymauyim), and is used by itself. "The Brown Driver and Briggs Hebrew and

English Lexicon" (BDB), doesn't combined them. I checked the commentaries of seven recognized modern scholars and none spoke of this "compound," making it 0 for 7. They were: F. F. Bruce, Merrill F. Unger, Allen P. Ross, Gleason L. Archer, C. I. Scofield, John MacArthur and Matthew Henry. Hugh Ross says, "The heavens and the earth," is a compound that, "refers uniquely to the totality of the physical universe, all its matter, energy, space and time." (Navigating Genesis, pp. 26-27). One problem with this interpretation is that neither Moses, nor his readers, would've understood what he wrote! If the heavens were where the birds fly locally and earth was a local land-area, he would've been clear. I believe Moses wrote to be understood! Despite God not being said to having spoken there, CMI thinks 1:1 is part of Day One and was the creation of "time, space and matter." Avery Foley (AIG), also thinks 1:1 is part of Day One and says, "the first thing He created was the earth." If "the earth" is visible in 1:1, why weren't "the heavens?" And why wasn't either called "very good," if this was an account of their creation? I see 1:2 referring to a local judgment because, darkness (Isa. 8:22, 2 Peter 2:17, Exo. 10:21-23) and a flood (Gen. 7:10) are judgments. And Isaiah 45:18 says, "For thus says Yahweh, Who created the heavens (He is the Eloheem Who formed the earth and made it, He established it and did not create it a waste place, but formed it to be inhabited). I Am Yahweh, and there is none else." Finally, Unger thought "heaven" in 1:1, referred to, "the immediate atmospheric heaven surrounding the earth, as the re-creative activity of the first four days suggests." (Unger p5). It's a small step from "atmospheric heaven surrounding the earth," to my, "local-atmosphere" below!

5. THE HEBREW WORD (SHAYMAUYIM), I TRANSLATE, "LOWER ATMOSPHERE," IS THE SAME

WORD USED FOR THE "AIR" WHERE THE BIRDS FLY IN GENESIS 1:26,27. One of the surest ways of reaching the truth in The Bible, is to let It interpret Itself by comparing Scriptures with Scriptures. I do that to reinforce many of my main points, when I delve into the meaning of Genesis One's statements. Genesis 1:6-8 says, "And God said, 'Let there be an expanse" (Hebrew, "raykeeag").' And God called the expanse, "shaymauyim." Genesis 1:7 tells us this "shaymauyim," had water above it (clouds containing water or just water of unknown thickness?) and below it (the deep). The point is: The word usually translated "heavens," as in "the heavens and the earth," cannot refer to the Universe. Further proof of this is shown on Day Four, when the Trinity "placed" the "two great lights" and "the stars" in the expanse of the lower atmosphere (shaymauyim) (Genesis 14-18). Unless you think the sun, moon and stars were created where the birds fly, it's only that their lights were made to "appear" in the lower atmosphere (heavens)from the standpoint of the Genesis One local area of land. In fact, you may be surprised to learn that neither the "sun" (shehmesh) nor the moon (yayhreehagh) are mentioned in Genesis One--only that their "lights" (mayhor) would rule. This local land area was recently judged, shown by the fact that Joel, (3:15), speaking of a future judgment, said, "The sun and moon grow dark and the stars lose their brightness." So Genesis One doesn't claim water, angels, Earth, the sun or the moon and stars were created during the time of Genesis. That the universe is billions of years old is shown by the fact that the light from many stars took billions of years to get here! John C. Whitcomb, Jr. And Henry M. Morris, (THE GENESIS FLOOD, p. 369), said, "The photons of light energy were created at the same instant as the stars from which they were apparently derived, so that an observer on the earth would have been able to see the most distant stars within his vision at the instant of creation." This statement is logically-incoherent! It's a statement with no scientific-backing! It takes eight minutes for the light from the sun to get here! Compare it with Hugh Ross: "Likewise, astronomers, through their observations of hyperfine spectral lines in distant stars and galaxies, have established that light's velocity has never varied throughout cosmic history." (Navigating Genesis, p. 161). On February 24, 1987, a supernova, 160,000 light years away was seen. At nearly the same time, thousands of trillions of neutrinos, passed through several neutrino detectors on Earth. So did these tiny particles also travel an unimaginable distance in no time?

6. THE HEBREW WORD (ERETZ) I TRANSLATE, " LAND," IS USED FOR THE "THE LAND OF NOD" (GENESIS 4:16), AND "THE LAND OF CANAAN" (GENESIS 13:12). THE REASON THE LOCAL LAND ISN'T NAMED IN 1:1 IS BECAUSE NOBODY LIVED THERE THEN. NO DISTINCTION WOULD'VE BEEN MEANINGFUL. On Day Three, God said, " 'Let the waters below the lower atmosphere be gathered into one place, and let dry ground appear;' and it was so." (1:9). BDB says "yabbhashah" means "dry ground" or "dry land." I go with "dry ground." In 1:10, "God called the dry ground, 'eretz.'" The land here cannot refer to the entire planet because then Moses would've included "the waters." This gathering of the waters, fixed the problem found in 1:2, where, the land "eretz" was hidden and useless (water, "the deep" hid the land's form, and made it useless-and-unseen). What's often translated, "Unformed," just means its form could not be seen! After all, everything that exists has a form. So I translate Genesis 1:2a, "The local land was 'hidden and useless'" (tohu wa-bohu). This makes sense because, when God fixed it by gathering "the water ... into one place" in 1:9, it went from

"hidden and useless" to "visible and useful." My translation is straight-forward, logical, easily-understood and literal. The Spirit of God is not said to be hovering over the "eretz," but rather the "deep." That the "waters" (the deep), are spoken of separately from "eretz," shows they are not part of this "eretz." Note: this condition in 1:2 was not good, nor called good. Why would God have created the land, He'd later dry up, under water? Why wouldn't He have created it above the water in the first place? In an earlier creation, found in Job 38, there was plenty of land not under water. So again, "In the beginning God revealed/fixed/arrayed the lower atmosphere and a local area of land." Genesis One is not about the original beginning and creation of the Universe. Also on day three, God "arrayed" the eretz with plants (1:11-12)..

7. THE WORD I TRANSLATE "WHEN" IN GENESIS 1:2, IS A "WAW DESCRIPTIVE" AND NOT A "WAW CONSECUTIVE," THEREFORE THE SCEENE IN 1:2 DESCRIBES THE SITUATION BEFORE 1:1. Scholars know, what is described in verse two does not follow consecutively after what's said in verse one. Other examples: "You will die because of the woman you have taken when she is married. She was already married "before" she was taken, (Gen. 20:3). "Shall I have pleasure, with my lord WHEN old?" (He was old "before" the question of pleasure, Gen. 18:12). "How can you say 'I love You," WHEN your heart is not with me?" (His heart was not with Him "before," he said, "I love.." Judges 16:15). In the same way, the land was covered with water in Gen. 1:2, "before" God "revealed/fixed/arrayed the lower atmosphere and the local land area" in 1:1.

Bruce K. Waltke (April, 1975), said, "The conjunctions introducing verses 2 and 3 are different in the original text. The waw introducing verse 3 does in fact denote sequence and is called by grammarians the "waw consecutive." But the waw introducing verse 2 is different in both form and function; grammarians refer to this waw as the 'waw conjunctive.' The waw conjunctive may introduce various types of clauses, but it does not introduce an independent sequential clause. It is inconceivable that Moses would have used a construction which does not indicate sequence in contrast to other constructions open to him, if this had been his intent." BDB concurs (p. 253). So 1:2 describes the situation in 1:1 and is not the results of what happened in 1:1.

Isaiah 45:18b tells us "He is God Who formed the land and made it. He established it and did not create it hidden and useless, but formed it to be inhabited." God confirmed this while questioning Job: "Where were you when I laid the foundation of the Earth? … And I placed boundaries on it … And I said, … 'here your proud waves shall stop.'" (Job 38: 4a, 10a, 11b). In an earlier creation, unlike in the Genesis beginning, there was land that could be seen and inhabited. So these other pertinent Scriptures tell us there were other creations before Genesis One. In Job's earlier creation, Earth's land isn't hidden and uninhabitable as we find it in Genesis 1:1-2 (I believe after a judgment of a previous local civilization). This is not to say there wasn't any dry land on Earth, when God removed water off a local land area (Gen. 1:1-2).

8. "THE GREAT DEEP (RAV TEHOM),IS NEVER USED IN CONNECTION WITH THE OCEAN ELSEWHERE IN THE BIBLE." It has been assumed that "the fountains of the great deep" (Gen. 7:1) referred to the depths of the ocean. But Isaiah 51:10 calls the place where the sea dried up for the redeemed to cross, the "great deep" (rav tehom). In his article: "The GISP2 Ice Core: Ultimate Proof that Noah's Flood Was Not Global," Paul H. Seely, said, "Since the ice sheet would've

floated away in the event of a global flood, the ice core is strong evidence that there was no global flood any time in the last 110,000 years." If Noah's flood couldn't be global, neither could the flood in 1:2.

9. SOLOMON SPOKE OF EARTH IN A BEGINNING THAT DIDN'T HAVE A DEEP, A GREAT DEEP OR WATER SPRINGS. He said, "From the beginning, from the earliest times of the Earth, when there were no depths ... when there were no springs filled with water." (Proverbs 8:23-24). This shows that there was a time in the early unjudged Earth, before Genesis, when it was waterless. The eternal Earth of the future will only have, "a river of the water of life, clear as crystal, coming from the thrown of God and of the Lamb," and no "sea" (Revelation 21:1, 22:1).

10. "THE SPIRIT OF GOD WAS HOVERING OVER THE SURFACE OF THE WATERS" (1:2b). The word "hovering" (raygrah), denotes fluttering in place, and is only used in two other OT places. Deuteronomy 32:11, speaks of an eagle,"that hovers over its young," and in Jeremiah 23:9 he tells us, "all my bones tremble." I believe The Spirit of God was hovering over the "Holy of Holies," on The Temple Mount. Oh, by the way, in case you're wondering if "the great sea monsters" (1:21), could've existed locally, the almost completely enclosed Mediterranean Sea has hundreds of whales. There are also whales in the Persian Gulf. Speaking of The Mediterranean Sea, near Haifa in Israel, 25-40 feet deep, is the megalith stone semicircle of Atlit Yam. These seven megaliths each weigh about 1,300 lbs.! Underground there, they found a 16-foot well and many well-preserved artifacts. This is possible evidence of the civilization destroyed in the 1:2 Flood. ("The 9,000-year-old underground megalithic settlement of

Atlit Yam," by April Holloway, 2020). Then there are the mysterious builders of the incredible complex of Gobekli Tempe, in Turkey! Built 10,000-11,500 years ago, "The central pair of (T-shaped pillas), of Enclosure D measure 5.5 m (@ 17 feet). and weigh about 8 to 10 metric tons each." ("How did they do it? Making and moving monoliths at Gobekli Tempe"), (internet).

11. ON THE FIRST DAY, GOD SEPARATED THE LIGHT (DAY) FROM THE DARKNESS (NIGHT), "AND THERE WAS EVENING AND THERE WAS MORNING: DAY ONE." (1:3-5). Again, this speaks of a local area of land. If it spoke of the entire globe, it would always be day and night somewhere and there would be many evenings and mornings each day. The flood and darkness, both point to the judgment of a previous civilization according to Genesis 7:19 and Exodus 10:21. There have been many previous civilizations on Earth. Neanderthals, Cro-Magnons, Denisovans, Clovis and others all lived BEFORE GENESIS. Over the years, I've seen science change their minds several times concerning, whether Neanderthals mated with our ancestors or not. In 2014 they said no, and in 2015 yes (Plos Biology, online). Those who believe we have DNA from Neanderthal mating, think it happened, 100,000 years ago, long BEFORE GENESIS. As for Cro-Magnons; In "Mapping Human History," (p. 29), Steve Olson said, "We have become somewhat smaller and lighter." In "Reflections of Our Past," (p. 145), John H. Relethford said, "Our bones are slightly less rugged and our teeth are slightly smaller." In Everything You Know is Wrong," (p.71), Lloyd Pye said they were, "taller than we are, averaging over six feet" and "their arm length was often a bit longer than ours." I would not expect their height or arm-length to be greater than ours!

Again, Cro-Magnons existed long BEFORE GENESIS! What I think has happened, is that when God created our race, He wanted us to be a little like Neanderthals and a lot like Cro-Magnons, which explains why we have DNA that looks like we mated with them. Secular scientists don't even consider that there might have been civilizations on Earth, long before us and unrelated to us.

12. THERE WAS NO DUST ON THE EARTH IN A BEGINNING BEFORE GENESIS. Genesis 2:7a says, "Then the Lord God formed man of the dust (gayfar) of the ground." But Solomon spoke of Earth in a beginning before Genesis, "From the beginning, from the earliest times of the Earth," when, God "had not yet made ... the first dust (gayfar) of the world." (Proverb 8:23,26).

13. GOD IS NOT SAID TO HAVE LAID THE FOUNDATIONS OF THE EARTH IN GENESIS. Job 38:4, Zechariah 12:1, and Psalm 104:5 all speak of "the foundations (yaysad) of the Earth," while Genesis doesn't. The Genesis beginning came sometime way after God's laying of the foundations of the Earth. The point here is that I accept the fact that Earth wasn't created in Genesis, only a local land mass was "revealed/fixed/arrayed." CMI thinks the entire planet was created in Genesis, despite the fact that, in their view, there's no place in Genesis where it tells us it was created. They think "ehretz" in 1:1 consists of the particles planet Earth would be made from and on Day Three when the water was gathered to one place "revealing" dry land. The reason God isn't shown to speak in the 1:1 beginning is because, the action doesn't start until verse three. Genesis 1:1 is just a statement of fact. God could have easily had Moses tell us He spoke in 1:1, but didn't choose to do so in order that we'd know it was just a statement of fact concerning two things that happened during the Six Days (God revealed/fixed/arrayed a local atmosphere and land area.)

14. WHEREAS GENESIS 1:1 IS A "STATEMENT OF FACT," "BEFORE" THE SIX DAYS, CONCERNING TWO THINGS THAT WERE REVEALED DURING THEM; 2:4 "IS A STATEMENT OF FACT" "AFTER" THEM, CONCERNING THE SAME TWO THINGS. In both places it refers to a local area where birds fly--"the heavens" (shayauyim), and a local area of "land" (eretz). And in both places it refers to the fact that they were "revealed." That the eretz (local land area), was only "revealed," or made to "appear," is clearly shown by the fact that it was only seen/revealed (raah), after the water was "gathered into one place." (1:9). Genesis 2:4 says, "This is the account of the heavens and the earth when they were revealed/fixed/arrayed in the day that the Lord God revealed/fixed/arrayed the local land and heavens." Since they refer to the same account, "bahrah" (created) in 1:1 and 2:4, and "gahsah" (made) also in 2:4 are used interchangeably. And since, at least eretz, was "revealed," we know "raah" was used interchangeably with "bahrah" and "gahsah." This also strengthens the belief that when God "made" (gahsah) the" two great lights ... and stars" (1:16), He only revealed them. The overwhelming scriptural and scientific evidence, tells us the planet Earth, and the sun, moon and stars were all here long BEFORE GENESIS and its Six Days a few thousand years ago! And Earth was not "created" before the sun as YEC believes!

15. NOAH'S FLOOD, IN MANY WAYS, WAS A REPLAY OF THE GENESIS ONE FLOOD. IN BOTH CASES FLOOD-WATER RECEDED FROM A LOCAL AREA OF LAND, WHERE LIFE WAS RESTORED (GENESIS CHAPTERS 1,6,7,8).

TEN

If Noah's Flood Was Local, It Points To A
Replay Of A Local Genesis 1:2 Flood

WAS NOAH'S FLOOD LOCAL OR GLOBAL? THAT IS THE IMPORTANT
question we will now explore! As the starting point, "all major
creationist organizations agree that it's far from possible that two of
every species on Earth today could've been on Noah's Ark." This is
well-known! So if they weren't on the Ark, how is it that they're here?
Proponents of the local flood think: "The reason the Earth is filled
with millions of species that weren't on the Ark is because, Noah's
Flood didn't reach to where they lived." Global flood organizations do
not believe any animals got here by evolving. They think: "The Earth
is filled millions of species that weren't on the Ark because various
KINDS of animals on the Ark, quickly produced them through
GENETIC VARIABILITY." So the debate comes down to these two
choices! If the Flood didn't reach beyond a local area, then it's easy to
understand how millions of the species living elsewhere, along with
the animals on the Ark, account for all of the species on Earth today.
Now let's see if "GENETIC VARIABILITY" could also do the job. If
it can't, the belief that a global Noah's Flood explains the vast majority
of Earth's geology, is dead! It also kills the thought that the Universe
was created in six days a few thousand years ago! Let's see! Though
YEC doesn't call this "quick change" in animal body plans, "evolution,"
evolutionists certainly would, if that's what they saw! Evolutionists

are always on the lookout for anything they can call, "evolution." If they ever found even one case of a "kind' that produced a "species," the entire world would know about it! If evolutionists ever did see it, they'd have a world-wide party! It would open the door wide, for the belief in evolution! But it has never happened! Nobody has ever seen it! Yet these same YEC people, claim we Ancient Earth Creationists leave the door open for evolution by admitting to a Universe and Earth created billions of years ago.

CAN THE "GENETIC VARIABILITY" OF A RELATIVELY FEW "KINDS" ON NOAH'S ARK, EXPLAIN THE MILLIONS SPECIES ON EARTH TODAY?

Thanks to the help of some of the world's top entomologists: James M. Carpenter and John W. Wenzel (yellowjackets), Thomas D. Seeley (honey bees), the late Robbin W. Thorpe (bumble bees), and my own personal observations, I've become something of an expert concerning these insects. I wrote 34 articles (with photos), about them for the Poughkeepsie Journal. If Noah's Flood was global, these insects couldn't be here, nor could any KIND of insect have produced them through "GENETIC VARIABILITY!" For one thing, bumble bees, yellowjackets and honey bees are so unalike that no imaginable insects could've produced any of them! That's true of the 20,000 bee species and 30,000 wasp species in the world! New York State's entomologist (yes we have one), Timothy McCabe, told me there are 13 yellowjacket species in the State. The only way that number can increase is if a different species moves in. There's no possibility evolution or "GENETIC VARIABILITY" could produce a new species with a different body-plan! From the Ark, the KINDS needed to produce these insects would've needed vast fields of flowers to produce the pollen/nectar/insects for food to keep them alive long enough for the so-called "GENETIC VARIABILITY" to take place? (Yellowjackets, wasps and hornets eat insects!). How many seeds would've survived the

YEC raging-global-flood, been planted near where the Ark landed and have grown in time so all the kinds of insects could've lived to produce offspring of any sort? How would any KIND of wasp or bee species be able to hide from birds that eat them? How could they feed the larvae of the new species? The logistics required are simply unimaginable after a horrific world-wide flood! And the fact is: nobody knows what the ancestors of any insect are, which makes it hard to believe there are any that arose from evolution or "GENETIC VARIABILITY!" Walk anywhere in nature and you'll never see either happening. If it ever happened, it should be happening now! There should be trillions of animals in the process of becoming a new species! The Bible doesn't have any kinds making species! Kinds and species are the same and God made them all to reproduce after their "kind" (species). If kind doesn't mean species, then there's no Old Testament word for species!

HOW DID ALL OF THE CATS GET HERE AFTER THE FLOOD

Let's look into whether it's logical or not to think all the cats on Earth today got here from two small cats on Noah's Ark as YEC proposes! Is it reasonable or unreasonable? Does it make sense or is it nonsense? Did Earth's 9 types of tigers, 7 types of lions, 34 jaguars subpopulations, 12 types of leopards, 6 cougars subspecies, 7 types of cheetahs, 3 snow leopard subspecies, 12 bobcat species, and 3 species of extinct saber-toothed cats (larger than lions), all arise rather quickly from two small cats through "GENETIC VARIABILITY" as the global flood believers think? The reason, for example, that nobody knows the non-lion ancestor or ancestors of lions is because, no such animals ever existed. If they had, then we'd expect to see some now! It's rather convenient to say they used to exist, but don't now! What we see and don't see is the most important factor when seeking the truth concerning how any animal got here! What is true of lions, also goes for all the big cats, which are so unalike as to make it unthinkable that "GENETIC VARIATION" could've made them all from two small cats on Noah's Ark, in the short time between then and now, like YEC demands! True a lion and a tiger can mate and make hybrids called ligers or tigons, which can also mate, but all of their offspring are sterile, leading to a dead end! And after producing these hybrids, both tigers and lions continue to exist. So if lions and tigers still exist, certainly we'd have to say it's reasonable to believe, their supposed never-seen, unknown ancestors, that also got here through "GENETIC VARIABILITY," would still be here producing more tigers and lions, instead of nobody having the slightest clue concerning what these supposed cats were!!?? To say something's "unreasonable," means, "No person being reasonable, would believe it!" Let's zero in on one animal--lions!

ARE LIONS THE RESULTS OF "GENETIC VARIABILITY?"

Since the example YEC uses to prove all the cats could've gotten here by "Genetic Variation," is that lions and tigers can mate and produce, ligers (lion is male) or tigons (tiger is male), which can in turn mate and have offspring, which are sterile! This scenario creates more problems than it solves! These hybrids have bodies that are part tiger and part lion, which, if a similar process produced lions, would mean lions, for example, were made by a male and a female that were different from one another. Lions show no sign of this at all! In fact, lions have been around since the time when Job lived (Job 4:10). And Job lived during the years of the Patriarchs, shown by the fact that he lived to an age similar to theirs. After raising two successive families, Job lived another 140 years (Job 42:16-17). The Alexandrian Septuagint adds to Job 42:16, saying he lived to 240. According to Bishop James Ussher's famous "The Annals of the World" (p. 26), God made a covenant with Abram (exalted father)and changed his name to Abraham (father of many) in 1897 BC. The fact that Job makes no mention of the Temple or Tabernacle, tells us he lived before Moses. When Jacob said "Judah is a lion's whelp" (Genesis 49:9), it was about 1689 BC. Since Noah's Flood ended in 2348 BC, 2 small cats had to have produced all of the cats that led to lions in less than 700 years. And as far as we know, there were always lions since the Genesis One creation??

ARE ALL THE BIRDS AND INSECTS HERE NOW DECENDANTS FROM NOAH'S ARK?

What about birds and insects? Did the over 11,000 bird species and over 900,000 insect species in the world arise from a few "kinds" on Noah's Ark? The Bible says, "No!" How so? Genesis 1:21 says, "God created ... every winged bird after their kind (min)." There's no mention of kinds (mins) of flying or hopping insects in Genesis One, which of course strongly points to only a local creation, with plenty of insects in nearby lands, already there before Genesis, ready to move in. Leviticus 11:13b-19 speaks of: "the eagle and the vulture and the buzzard and the kite and the falcon in its kind (min), every raven in its kind (min), and the ostrich and the owl and the sea gull and the hawk in its kind (min), and the little owl and the cormorant and the great owl, and the white owl and the pelican and the carrion vulture, and the stork, the heron in its kind (min), and the hoopoe and the bat." Then 11:22b speaks of: "the locust in its kind (min), and the devastating locust in its kind (min), and the cricket in its kind (min), and the grasshopper in its kind (min)." Note that there are even two different "kinds" (mins) of locusts! It's not that one "kind" made all of the "species" of locusts, as would be expected in the "Genetic Variability" hypothesis! If there are two "kinds" of locusts, we're back to Noah's Ark having to contain far more animals than it possibly could! You may also suppose one "kind" of insect made crickets and grasshoppers; but each is called a "kind" (min) here. And at the very least, falcons, ravens and hawks are different "kinds (mins)," despite being quite alike in the bird kingdom! Can "Genetic Variability" be a thing that produces new species and the only people who know of it are those who think Noah's Flood was global and the Universe was created in six days a few thousand years ago?!? The belief doesn't make sense and therefore to believe it is "nonsense!" Yes! Problem # one for evolution and for "Genetic Variation," is: "That's not what we see! If we believe our eyes, we know new species are not seen in the process of being made!

ARE ALL THE LAND SNAKES ON EARTH DECENDANTS FROM NOAH'S ARK?

Did a few snakes on Noah's Ark produce all of the varieties of snakes here now? They've recently found the skeleton of a "titanboa," that was 50 feet long and weighed 2,500 pounds! Scientists think they lived 58 million years ago! Did they live that long ago, or were they made since Noah's Ark? Were there snakes with fangs on the Ark, or are we to believe, fangs arose quickly since the Flood? If poison snakes with fangs were on the Ark, what stopped them from killing other animals? Same goes for snakes that kill by strangulation.

NOAH'S FLOOD AND THE FOUNTAINS OF THE GREAT DEEP (VOLCANISM AND NOAH'S FLOOD)

Early in Noah's flood, "all the fountains of the great deep burst open" (Gen. 7:11). YEC consider this to be a huge volcanic event. They use this to explain much of the world's extremely thick and widespread lava rocks conventional science tells us took millions of years to form. If all of that volcanism took place in and around Noah's Flood, the ocean would've been poisoned far beyond what would've killed all aquatic life. But anyway, only "the water increased" (7:17). Isaiah 30:33 speaks of "a stream of fire and brimstone." No such stream is spoken of in conjunction with Noah's flood. All of Earth's extreme volcanism took place long BEFORE GENESIS, just as conventional science says. The "Deccan Traps," layers (from one volcano), formed 66 million years ago and cover 200,000 square miles to a depth of 1.2 miles! That's 122,750 cubic miles! Common sense science tells us that volcano erupted for 30,000 years, whereas YEC wants us to believe those square miles and most of Earth's other huge layers were laid during or around 150 days (Gen. 7:24-8:2), when the "fountains of the great deep" were open!?!? Imagine how intense the explosion that laid the Deccan Traps would've been in order to lay 200,000 square miles of magma in around 150 days!! And remember, the fish lived and Noah's Ark wasn't rocked enough during those 150 days to even cause seasickness?!?!

The Hebrew word "*magyahn*," translated "fountains" in 7:11 and 8:2, appears 23 times in the O. T. and "water" is the only substance ever associated with it. There is no Biblical authority to insert volcanism into this context. At the end of the flood, "the fountains of the deep and the floodgates of the sky were closed" (8:2). Just as the only things to "burst open" in "the great deep" were water "fountains," the only things God closed in "the deep" at the end were water "fountains." Nothing else in the deep is said to open or close! To add volcanism, is to add to the Word of God. Once God "closed" the opening in the great deep, He is not said to reopen it. Since none of the Flood water was said to return to an opening in the great deep, it points to a local flood because, if it was global, certainly some of its water would be expected to return inside the Earth, otherwise where could it all have gone?

The above is more-or-less a moot-point because, the "great deep" (rav tehom), when referring to a place, is only found in one other scripture! Amos 7:4 says, "Thus Yahweh (God) showed me, and behold, Yahweh was calling to contend by fire, and it consumed the great deep (rav tehom) and began to consume the farm land." Obviously "rav tehom" here, refers to a local body of water nowhere near the size or location of the bottom of the ocean! To call "rav tehom" the bottom of the ocean in the Genesis Flood story, is based on a non-Biblical assumption.

MOUNTAINS RISING DURING NOAH'S FLOOD

YEC proposes that the mountains were made high, some say, when the continents collided late in Noah's flood. But Genesis tells us the "high mountains" were already there before the flood. "The water prevailed more and more upon the land, so that all the high mountains everywhere under the local heavens were covered." (7:19). Then after "the water receded" (8:3), "the tops of the mountains became visible." (8:5). This is not a picture of mountains being pushed up by huge earth-shaking collisions as YEC science teaches. If Earth's mountains rose during Noah's Flood, the resulting tsunamis would've, at least rocked the ark, harming the animals. Had the mountains been blasted up much higher, they would've appeared **before** "the water receded!" So there is no record of mountains being forced up in Genesis. Without a doubt, if such huge events happened during the time of Genesis, it would've told us so. The prophecy of Jeremiah 4:24 says, "I looked on the mountains, and behold they were quaking, and all the hills moved to and fro." Certainly Genesis would've told us if something similar took place during Noah's flood. Since it bothered to tell us, "all the fountains of the great deep burst open," it wouldn't make sense not to speak of other catastrophic events, if they had taken place. To add mountain-rising during Noah's Flood, is to add to the Word of God.

The only Scripture I've seen YECs use to prove the mountains rose during Noah's flood is Psalm 104: 6-8 (NASB): "The waters were standing above the mountains. At Your rebuke they fled, at the sound of Your rebuke they fled, at the sound of Your thunder they hurried away. The mountains rose; the valleys sank down ..." Note that it is only after the waters "hurried away" that "The mountains rose; the valleys sank down," matching the Genesis account, which had no catastrophe other than a flood. I believe this is **PHENOMENAL LOGICAL LANGUAGE**, just as in two verses earlier in 104:22 where it says: "the sun rises." The sun doesn't actually rise, the Earth spins! The KJV doesn't even say, 'The mountains rose,' but rather: "They

(the waters) go up by the mountains; they go down by the valleys ..."
(Psalm 104:8). The NIV says, "They flowed over the mountains, they
went down into the valleys." We do not have a mountain-raising event
mentioned in either Genesis or Psalm 104.

CONTINENTAL DRIFT AND NOAH'S FLOOD

YEC also teaches the world's one-time single great continent, Pangaea,
split and ran across the ocean in conjunction with Noah's flood,
without causing a tsunami strong enough to destroy the ark or make the
residents seasick? The online article, *"What About Continental Drift?"*
(ChristianAnswers.net), says, "The model proposed by Baumgardner
begins with a pre-flood super-continent ("Let the waters be gathered
into one place" Genesis 1:9) ... At its peak, this thermal instability
would have allowed for subduction at rates of meters-per-second. This
key concept is called runaway subduction." One point they're trying
to make here is that when there was only one continent, the waters
were, "gathered into one place." In this way they think they've proven
this "continental drift" took place "after the Six Days," by saying, "The
waters were no longer in *one place* because, there was no longer just
one continent, thanks to continental-drift during Noah's Flood." But
science tells us there's only one ocean now! The *National Oceanic and
Atmospheric Administration* says, "All of the Earth's oceans exchange
water, so technically there is only one global ocean." *Universe Today*
says, "From the scientific point of view there is only one major ocean
called the World Ocean." The *National Geographic Society* says, "There
is one ocean." At the very least, YEC hasn't proven their point here.
What we SEE is that "Continental-Drift" moves at the same speed as
our fingernails grow! Occam's razor tells us the vast majority of the
continental-drift took place over millions of years. To say that the there
was only one continent a few thousand years ago, and during Noah's
Flood that continent broke apart and drifted to the places where
continents are now, is to add to the Word of God again. Why doesn't

Genesis tell us about the breaking apart of a one-world-continent and the fast-drifting of its sections across the globe, if that took place during Noah's Flood? How many ultra-huge, Earth-shattering events can we expect Noah's Ark to have survived? How is it the animals in the Ark weren't thrown around and injured? How is it nobody even got seasick?

In a way the above points are moot because, "the great deep" (never refers to the ocean anywhere else in the Bible.

METEORITES AND NOAH'S FLOOD

To make matters impossibly-worse, YEC **uses its science** in an attempt to prove there was an ultra-huge meteorite event in conjunction with Noah's Flood. But Genesis only tells us: " ...the floodgates of the sky were opened and the fountains of the great deep were opened. The rain fell upon the earth for forty days and forty nights." (Gen. 7:11,12). Nothing else is said to have come out of the sky nor from the Earth. Had huge impact events taken place during and/or right before or after Noah's flood, as YEC teach, we would expect many to have been killed by its effects. But Genesis 6:17 says, "Behold I, even I Am bringing the flood of water upon the earth, to destroy all flesh in which is the breath of life, from under heaven; everything that is on earth shall perish." Jesus said, " ...the flood came and destroyed them all." (Luke 17:27). None are said to die in any other way.

Michael J. Oard, a board member of THE CREATION RESEARCH SOCIETY (CRS), wrote an article in THE CREATION MINISTRIES INTERNATIONAL (CMI): JOURNAL OF CREATIONISM (JOC) 23 (3) 61-69; titled: "HOW MANY IMPACT CRATERS SHOULD THERE BE ON EARTH?" YEC admits that by using moon data, there should be about 36,000 over 30 km. (about 14 miles in diameter), about 100 greater than 500 miles in diameter and a few 2,000 to 2,500 miles in diameter on Earth. "This bombardment must have occurred very early in the flood, tailing off during the rest of the flood with a few post-flood impacts. Such a bombardment would be adequate to initiate the Flood. The evidence for such an impact bombardment very likely can be found in the precambrian igneous rocks and suggests that the precambrian is early Flood ... If even a small fraction of the 36,000 impacts occurred after the Flood (as well as before the Flood), all biology would have been wiped out ... In regard to possible impacts before the Flood, I accept W. R. Spencer's analysis (Deyoung, CRS Quarterly) that the solar system was created with no impact structures. This seems logical to me, since everything was created very good and meteorite bombardments do not seem to be very good phenomenon, especially if there were organisms living on the earth at the time."

Oard added, "Another subtle piece of evidence probably is ultra high-pressure minerals and micro-diamonds found in mountains all over the world can be formed by impacts. Otherwise the alternative is to rapidly push continental rocks well below 100 km. And then rapidly exume them, presenting a conundrum, especially for uniformitarians." Well I think that's a conundrum for anyone who thinks that happened in conjunction with the short period during and around Noah's Flood, without The Bible mentioning any meteors falling from the sky? When they conflict, the Bible must always trump our science. So I'm calling for YEC to: **"Give up your science that adds to The Bible and accept The Scriptures as they are; without meteorites, excessive volcanism, an ice age, or continental drift during Noah's Flood and the years just before and after it." Real science confirms what The Bible says and what it doesn't say. Real science confirms that the majority of Earth's massive volcanism, its 36,000 meteorite impacts, the history of continental-drifts and Ice Ages all took place long BEFORE GENESIS.**

Fellow YEC, Rod Bernitt of CMI (JOC 24 (1), 2010), responded to Oard's article. His letter to the editor was rather baffling. First he calls it an "excellent article," and then proceeds to do a great job of debunking its main premise!?!? Bernitt said, "If the duration of the impacts is restricted to 40 days (Genesis 7: 11-12), how does the earth avoid becoming a large, magma ocean over much of its surface? Another concern, how does the Ark with Noah and all on board avoid asteroid generated tidal waves? 36,000 or more asteroid impacts with an average size and kinetic energy as I used, may generate hundreds, even thousands of tidal waves."

Michael J. Oard responded to Bernitt: "There is the possibility that the impacts could have occurred at creation. But this does not seem likely since the moon was created on Day 4, meaning that a lot of plants would have been destroyed on the earth if all the impacts were on day 4. Of course, impacts after Day 4 would have destroyed a lot of animals in God's 'very good' creation." (And death in the new creation can't be before sin!)

By combining the statements of these two high-profile YECs, we find the huge Earth-wrecking-asteroids known to have impacted the Earth, haven't done so at least 36,000 times during or after the Six Days of Genesis! *All of these impacts happened in the ages "before" Genesis, which explains why Genesis is silent concerning them.*

Mainstream scientists do believe in catastrophism. In fact, they usually believe the catastrophies, like Ice Ages, impact craters, and volcanism were far worse and happened more often than YEC does. I only point this out because YEC likes to criticize modern scientists for attributing the Earth's history almost all to "uniformitarianism."

In the online article, "Debunking Scientific Evidence for a Global Flood" Part 1-- "Fossil meteorites and impact craters in the geological column," it lists 157 impact craters in the geological column, between the present and two billion year years ago, including the layer they're in. How could impact craters form miles below the Flood waters? Then in a limestone quarry in Sweden dating to the Ordovician (485 to 443 million years ago), 101 fossilized meteorites were found (100 more than is to be expected in such a small area). YEC statements saying the expected meteorite evidence is not in the geologic column are false.

Dust from the enormous meteor impact or impacts that formed

the "iridium layer," was laid long BEFORE GENESIS. If that dust was blasted into the air during Noah's Flood, it would've been scattered and mixed with the waters instead of having laid a distinct layer. Science says it was 66 million years ago, long BEFORE GENESIS, when the six-mile wide asteroid caused an impact crater 12 miles deep and 110 miles in diameter.

NOAH'S FLOOD AND THE ICE-AGE/ICE-AGES

The reason there are no Ice-Ages in Genesis is because they took place BEFORE GENESIS! Nobody except YECs think there was an Ice-Age that only lasted 500-700 years less than 8,000 years ago. The ice sheets were two miles deep over New York State! Genesis doesn't even say it got cold! The Ice-Ages were BEFORE GENESIS! The last Ice -Age lasted about 110,000 years and ended 11,500 years ago. The Huronian Ice-Age(the largest of the five known), lasted from 720 to 630 million years ago. There are three signatures ancient glaciers left behind: (1) striations, (2) tillites, (3) dropstones.

NOAH'S FLOOD AND CORAL REEFS

Certainly no coral reefs could've lived through the immense volcanism global flood believers claim happened! Let alone all of the asteroids, continental-drift, and the surging flood-waters they claim formed the Grand Canyon! "The Great Barrier Reef Surprisingly Young (New geological data point to age of less than a million years) by Ben Harder for "Science." "Stretching for 1,429 miles over an area of approximately 133,000 square miles, the Great Barrier Reef is the largest coral reef system in the world." ("What is the Great Barrier Reef," NOAA service website, https://oceanservice.noaa.gov/facts/eutro phication. html, 01/20/23). The Chazy Fossil Reef is 480 million years old and covers 1,567 acres and spans three Lake Champlain islands in Clinton

County, New York and Grand Isle County, Vermont. "Chazy Fossil Reef" (Wikipedia, online).

NOAH'S FLOOD AND THE GEOLOGICAL COLUMN

Genesis does not have anything that went on, and certainly not Noah's Flood, that could explain the huge geological-layers. Ronald L. Numbers relates that geologists believe, "it takes 6,000 years to lay an inch of limestone." (*The Creationists*, p. 236). Francis D. Nichol, a Seventh-day Adventist, said, "It has always been something of a perplexity to me to visualize just *how* amid the turbulence of the Flood and the period of subsidence immediately following, there would be sufficient opportunity for one stratum to take definite and distinctive shape and mold before another was hurled upon it by the restless ebb and flow of the waters." (p. 113). Hugh Ross said, "In the 1780s, Abraham Werner showed that silt and rocks are deposited in beds or formations in successive layers." (*CREATION AND TIME* p. 27). "Georges Cuvier and Jean Lamark noted that particular fossils relate to particular strata. Subsequently, geologists d'Orbigny, Lyell, Hall, and Hutton concluded from their calculations of geological deposition rates that life must have existed on Earth for at least a quarter of a billion years, with significant, progressive changes over that time. Most geologists of the day made no claims that life made these changes on its own. Those who stated their hypotheses typically proposed that God had responded to various cosmic and terrestrial catastrophes (e.g., asteroid collisions, volcanoes, ice ages, etc.) with **separate, successive creations.**" (p. 28).

Note that these scientists believed in "**successive creations**," which makes it much more difficult to believe in evolution because, then life would've had to have begun and evolved many times. Evolutionists are not saying Earth is billions of years old just to leave room for evolution. It's what they SEE in the Earth's crust.

Does The Bible teach that all of the many miles of geological layers were laid during Noah's Flood? The "olive leaf" will help us answer this question! But first we'll look at two birds!

THE RAVEN AND THE DOVE

Genesis 8:7-12 says: "And he sent out a raven, and it flew here and there until the water was dried up from the earth. Then he sent out a dove from him to see if the water was abated from the face of the land. But the dove found no resting place for the sole of her foot, so she returned to him into the ark, for the water was on the surface of all the earth. Then he put out his hand and took her into the ark to himself. So he waited yet another seven days; and again he sent out the dove from the ark. The dove came to him toward evening, and behold in her beak was a freshly picked olive leaf. So Noah knew that the water was abated from the earth. Then he waited yet another seven days, and sent out the dove, but she did not return to him again."

The raven represents restless people who seek satisfaction everywhere except for the one place it can be found--in the center of God's will! The raven was probably sent out first because, it was by the window, longing to be somewhere besides in God's will, even though He was kind to it by preserving its life. The fact that the raven found no place to rest didn't stop it from searching and searching and searching! Determine to do your own will and see where that takes you? It always leads to a wasted life, full of regrets and ultimately to eternal despair. Isaiah said, "The wicked are like the tossing sea" (Isa. 57:20). Solomon said "The way of the wicked is like darkness; they do not know over what they stumble." (Proverbs 4:19). Job 20:5 says, "The triumphing of the wicked is short, and the merry-making of the Godless momentary."

The dove represents those who've learned, like Noah, to trust God, Who always takes care of us in every way. I'm sure Noah longed to feel the sunshine on his body, the good earth beneath his feet and the cool wind against his face; but he had learned to wait patiently for God's timing in everything. No wonder, "Noah found grace in the eyes of the Lord." (Gen. 6:8). Though Noah was in a difficult situation; being cooped up and having a lot of animals to care for, yet he was in the best place in the universe! He was in God's will. Are you in the best place in the universe at this moment? If you're a Christian and you don't think so, you must think either God doesn't know what He's doing or He doesn't love you. Are your eyes opened to see "that God causes all things to work together for good to those who love God, to those who are called according to His purpose." (Romans 8:28). Many are like Jacob, who said, "God was in this place and I did not know it." (Gen. 28:16).

Can it be that you expected a nice easy, peaceful life; while Jesus and the Apostles had many trials, hardships and troubles? Jesus said, "These things I have spoken to you, so that in Me you may have peace, In the world, you have tribulation, be of good courage; I have overcome the world." (John 16:33). The Apostle Paul said we should be "rejoicing in hope, persevering in tribulation, devoted to prayer." (Romans 12:12).

THE OLIVE LEAF AND NOAH'S FLOOD

On page 40 of *Biblical Creationism*, famed YEC author, Henry M. Morris, tells us, "The returning dove had found that plant life had begun to grow on the land again, presumably from seeds or cuttings carried by the waters until deposited on the earth's surface, so Noah knew the animals could find food to eat ..." It seems to me, since seven days earlier "water was on the surface of all the earth" (Gen. 8:9), the dove with "a freshly picked olive leaf ... in her beak" (8:11), shows us the leaf didn't come from "seeds or cuttings." This points to a pre-flood tree still growing where it was before the Flood. All of the volcanic ash and lava, the limestone, sandstone, clay, shale, salt, coal and topsoil required in the YEC Flood models, would've mixed with the raging ocean water to make a soup far too toxic to expect a quick fig leaf if any at all. If all of the impact craters, volcanism, and continental-drifts and collisions took place in conjunction with Noah's flood, as YEC believes, we would expect all or almost all of the seeds and cuttings to be either destroyed or buried somewhere deep under the up to 25 miles of geological layers. Yes they believe that in places about 25 miles of various types of sandstone. limestone, shale and basalt (lava-rocks), according to *answers In Genesis* (AIG), were laid down in 119 layers atop of the world that existed before the flood. Cuttings, if any made it through the Flood, poisoned by unimaginable amounts of magma etc., would take more than a few days to grow roots and make fig leaves, if they could grow at all after the Flood in the YEC model. So upon closer look, the hypothesis that much of the Earth's geology can be attributed to Noah's Flood, simply cannot hold Flood water!

DINOSAURS AND **NOAH'S FLOOD**

Based on what The Bible teaches concerning the size of the Ark, no creationist scholar I know of thinks there was any possibility that two of all of the land animals in the entire world were on the Ark. Science, for example knows of 500 distinct genera and more than 1,000 species of non-avian dinosaurs. AIG says, "Although there are about 668 names of dinosaurs, there are perhaps only 55 different "kinds" of dinosaurs. Furthermore, not all dinosaurs were huge like the Brachiosaurus and even those dinosaurs on the ark were probably "teenagers" or young adults." So by their own admission, YEC, like everybody else, knows all of the species alive today couldn't have been on the Ark. They think at least 110 dinosaurs were on the ark (two each of the 55). and since new types of dinosaurs are constantly being found, who knows how many more? Now let's say those 55 "kinds," supposedly aboard the Ark, survived but didn't breed in such a way as to bring back the 945+ distinct species not on the ark. That would mean either "two of all of 668+species of dinosaurs were on the ark, or that many existed when the 55 pairs on the Ark were through producing new species?? In this model, Noah's Flood would've brought most of them to extinction, which is what the Ark was supposed to prevent. To feed, exercise and clean up after at least 110 "teenage" dinosaurs, not to mention the myriads of other "kinds" of animals, already points the utter impossibility of a global Noah's Flood. Then of the 110, several had to be meat-eaters! What prevented them from eating the other Ark-animals? YEC cannot find a Biblical answer, because there isn't one! Many think they hibernated, but that's adding to The Word of God!

BUMBLE BEES, HONEY BEES AND NOAH'S FLOOD

Though bumble bees are tough, even fierce animals; yet they cannot survive without a delicate combination of proper weather and acceptable habitat. On or off the ark, their life-cycle wouldn't allow them to survive a world-wide flood lasting as long as Noah's. Male bumble bees do not live through winter because they cannot hibernate. So why would God include them in the animals (**male** and female), He brought into the ark? The only bumble bees needed are the potential new queens. These are fertilized females that "become" queens once some of their larvae become worker bees for them to reign over. They hibernate in dirt and will die of hypothermia if they are too wet for too long. In order for their species to survive, they must have a viable source of nectar and pollen upon emergence from hibernation. Timing is crucial! They will starve if they're forced to remain in hibernation too long or cannot find enough flowers and/or tree blossoms after emerging from hibernation. I cannot see any possible way they could survive, having to depend on blossoms from cuttings and seeds (if any could even grow after the supposed poison volcanism required in YEC flood models). Nor can it be expected that enough flowers could bloom fast enough from seeds that floated around in poisonous water to feed the bumble bees in time to keep them alive. Even if the water somehow was fine despite all the volcanism, we cannot expect enough seeds to land, plant themselves, and grow within a few miles of the ark as the bumble bees would require.

These bumble bees would have to overcome extreme competition for nectar and pollen, including thousands of other types of bees, numerous species of yellowjackets, wasps and hornets. How do we know there were so many of these insect species? Simply because, they're all here now and could not be here unless they were around immediately "after" the flood.

Honey bees would've posed another even greater problem for any global-flood model. First of all, unlike other bees, they couldn't survive if only one fertilized female entered the ark. And there's no account of them or any kind of animal entering en mass. They do not hibernate and can only survive when there are thousands in a colony, within a closure, with enough honey for all to eat until the spring flowers became available. A single male and female entering the ark together would've been absolutely useless! Of all animals on Earth, honey bees may be the strangest and most talented, this despite the fact (entomologists tell us), that, like other insects they cannot reason. Well, Somebody reasoned! All of the grazing animals also would've been competing for many of the flowering plants.

BUTTERFLIES, MOTHS AND NOAH'S FLOOD

The vast majority of the 15,000+ kinds of butterflies and the 12,000+ kinds of moths, have life-cycles of much fewer days than the amount Noah's flood lasted. And how did they get on the Ark in the first place? They couldn't fly in as adults because, the vast majority only live a few months or less. They couldn't crawl in as caterpillars because, most kinds must spin cocoons on or near the plants they feed on. They'd die if they had to crawl into the Ark because, if by freak chance they could make it, they would lack the energy to spin a cocoon. But it's a moot point anyway because, as stated above, if the Flood was global, the vast majority, if not all, butterflies and moths would've gone extinct, not having enough time to complete their life-cycles before enough flowers bloomed. In fact, it wouldn't even be a close call. They would require flowering fields within 6-8 months after spinning a cocoon, and the fields were not ready for over 10 months. (Gen. 7:11, 8:14). Then there would've had to have been many "kinds" because the wing shapes, sizes, coloring and patterns God "painted" are so varied!

NOAH'S FLOOD AND THE IMMENSE AMOUNT OF INSECTS

Even if right before Noah's Flood, there was only one giant continent, basically containing all of the land masses on Earth now (as YEC believes), the account of two of every kind of insect flying or crawling into the ark, is not in Genesis. And none could've survived outside the Ark, in the terrifying flood YEC claims Noah's was!

ELEVEN

WE MUST TURN TO EZEKIEL 28 TO SEE A MAJOR REASON WHY SO many Bible scholars have claimed the universe and Earth were already ancient by the time of the six days of Genesis One. As an introduction to our study, we will turn to Merrill F. Unger: "This revelation is made under the king of Tyre because of the very close connection between human government of the fallen world system and Satan and the powers of darkness as the superhuman agencies, who are the real actors behind the scenes (cf. Dan. 10:13, where 'the prince of the kingdom of Persia' is really an evil spirit ruler) described in Ephesians 6:12 under the category 'the rulers of the darkness of this world,' literally, 'age rulers of this darkness.'" (*UNGER'S COMMENTARY ON THE OLD TESTAMENT P.* 1553). *Origen (c. 225 AD)* said, "What is said about the ruler of Tyre cannot be understood of a certain man who ruled over Tyre." (*Ante-Nicene Fathers* p. 4372). *Tertullian (c. 210AD)* said, "For in the person of the prince of Tyre, it says things in reference to the devil." (p. 3305). Let's see why what is said to this king in Ezekiel's lamentation, cannot be about him. Rather it is meant to show him, and us, that even the greatest, most wonderful and most fortunate being ever created could somehow become dissatisfied to the point where pleasing God no longer was his goal. He wanted to set out on his own! He wanted to please himself! He thought he could plan his life better than God could. He had to try something new! He somehow lost the knowledge, "that God causes all things to work together for good to those who love God, to those who are called according to purpose." (Romans 8:28). He had more talent, power, wisdom, and knowledge than any other being God ever created and a higher position. Now he exists in turmoil, restlessness, and extreme fear, knowing he will soon be tied up with a "great chain" and put in solitary-confinement in "the abyss" for "a thousand years" (Rev. 20:1-3), after which he will be thrown into **The Eternal Lake of Fire** (Revelation 20:10). Concerning these last days we're in, Revelation 12:12 says, "Woe to the earth and the sea, because the devil has come down to you, having great wrath, knowing that he has a short time." Since I believe everyone should read this at least once--here is Ezekiel 28: 11-19 and the greatest fall from grace ever anywhere in the universe. Here is an account of the very first sin.

Again the word of the Lord came to me saying, "Son of man, take up an intense anguish over the king of Tyre and say to him, 'Thus says the Lord God, "You had the seal of perfection, full of wisdom and perfect in beauty. You were in Eden, the garden of God; every precious stone was your covering: the ruby, the topaz the diamond, the beryl, the onyx, the jasper, the lapis lazuli, the turquoise, and the emerald. The workmanship of gold in your settings and sockets was in you. On the day you were created they were prepared. You were the anointed cherub who covers and I placed you there. You were on the holy Mountain of God. You walked in the midst of the stones of fire. You were perfectly blameless in all your ways from the day you were created until unrighteousness was found in you. By the abundance of your travel to trade and spread slanderous gossip you were internally filled with violence and you sinned. Therefore I have cast you as profane from the mountain of God. And I have destroyed you, O covering cherub from the midst of the stones of fire. Your heart was lifted up because of your beauty;. You corrupted your

wisdom by reason of your splendor. I cast you to the ground. I put you before kings that they may see you. By the multitude of your iniquities--in the unrighteousness of your trade and slanderous gossip, you profaned your sanctuaries. Therefore I have brought fire from the midst of you. It has consumed you and I have turned you to ashes on the earth. All who know you among the peoples are appalled at you. You have become terrified and will be gone forever."

1. Having the "seal of perfection" and being "perfectly blameless in all your ways," speaks of a long period of time and cannot refer to any human. Even Adam and Eve, before they sinned, weren't "perfect." They had to obey, resist and grow before they could become "perfect." They were sinless, but were not perfect. Perfection requires time!

2. Being "full of wisdom," also requires a long time. Job said, "Wisdom is with aged men, as is understanding." (Job 12:12).

3. I think he was on Earth when he became proud and sinned. I will ascend above the clouds. Unless it's cloudy in heaven! Even if it were cloudy in heaven, we would expect the throne to be in the main place (like Earth is here), and the clouds above.

4. I think He and his angels have been on Earth for at least many millions and possibly a billion years! They've had time to develop great technology, which we see in the world's pyramids and in the vast array of UFOs! It's even very possible they started out on Mars? Carl Sagon put forth the possibility that all civilizations destroy themselves with nuclear weapons (COSMOS p.251). Sagon also included a picture of the Pyramids of Elysium on Mars, and said they "warranted a careful look." (COSMOS p. 108). When John E. Brandenburg, Ph. D. (DEATH ON MARS p.109), told a nuclear physicist, "xenon 129 was superabundant in Mars atmosphere, compared to other isotopes, I mentioned He frowned deeply, and

then looked very troubled. 'Somebody nuked them,' he said suddenly.'" Were the angels on Mars when it's said of God, "He stretches out the north over empty space and hangs the Earth on nothing." (Job 26:7). At that time, "the morning stars sang together and all the sons of God (angels), shouted for joy." (Job 38:7). NASA's Curiosity Rover found a strange rectangular opening that looks like a doorway! Were Lucifer and his angels here at the time of the, perfectly-round metal-spheres, "found in pyrophylite, which is mined near the little town of Ottosdal in Western Transvaal" (South Africa). The pyrophylite was formed, "about 2.8 billion years ago." These spheres "are very hard and cannot be scratched, even by steel." "At least one," (of the many hundreds found), "has three parallel groves running around its equator." Roelf Marx, curator of the museum of Klerksdorp, South Africa, where some of the spheres are housed, said, "The spheres are a complete mystery. They look man-made, yet at the time in Earth's history when they came to rest in this rock no intelligent life existed." Or so they thought! "They're nothing like I have seen before." (Hidden History of the Human Race, by Michael A. Cremo and Richard L. Thompson, pp. 120-121). The internet, (Case For The Grooved Spheres, by James Barton), says they are about "one inch in diameter." "It also seems that the spheres are so delicately balanced that, even in modern technology, they would need to have been made in zero gravity."

5. Lucifer was Earth's first High Priest. He was in "Eden, the garden of Eloheem; every precious stone was your covering." Ezekiel 28:13 continues by nine of the 12 stones on the Jewish High Priest's robe (LXX provides the other 3). In any case, Lucifer was in an ancient Eden, where he "walked among the stones of fire" (Ez. 28:14) which was far different from Adam and Eve's Eden, which was full of plants!

6. Lucifer was the first King of Earth, shown by the fact that he had a throne (Isaiah14:13). He still is king of this cosmos (Matt. 4:8-9)

7. Lucifer was Earth's first Prophet. Exodus 24:10 says, "And they saw the Eloheem of Israel; and under His feet there appeared to be a pavement of sapphire, as clear as the sky." This is thought to correspond with "the stones of fire" Lucifer "walked among" (Ezekiel 28:14). In addition, he was "on the Holy Mountain of God" (Ez. 28:14).

8. Lucifer spent a long time gaining wealth using, "unrighteous trade and slanderous gossip." (Ez. 28:16).

JESUS SPOKE OF, "THE ETERNAL LAKE OF FIRE WHICH HAS BEEN PREPARED FOR THE DEVIL AND HIS ANGELS" (MATTHEW 25:41).

This speaks of a long time between when Lucifer sinned and when Adam and Eve did; otherwise this "eternal lake of fire would've also been prepared for all the people who failed to trust Christ for their salvation!

THERE ARE ELDERS OF THE UNIVERSE

In Revelation 5:8-10, we find 24 elders talking about those Christ "purchased" with His "blood." These elders say, "You have made THEM a kingdom and priests to our God and THEY will reign upon the Earth (5:10). The elders do not include themselves among the "purchased" and therefore they cannot be elders of the church or of Israel. Hebrews 1:13 and 12:2 have Jesus "seated" at God's right hand; but Acts 7:55 and Revelation 5:6 have Him "standing?" Any ideas why this is--contact me! Could it be that Jesus is usually seated; but stood when His beloved servant Stephen, the first Christian martyr, was being stoned to death for preaching and when John was taken to heaven to receive the Revelation? Stephen, by the way, prayed that God would forgive those who stoned him, thus obeying Jesus, Who said, "Love your enemies and pray for those who persecute you." (Matt. 5:44), and "Love your enemies, do good to those who hate you, bless those who curse you and pray for those who mistreat you." (Luke 6:27-28). While being crucified, Jesus said, "Father forgive them; for they do not know what they are doing." (Luke 23:34). For now I can only say, at the time of Revelation, He was standing and the elders were seated on thrones (4:4). Nobody in the church can be seated on a throne, while the Lamb is standing. Besides, at the time of Revelation, the rapture hadn't happened! So my point is that there are elders (angels?), that are even older than the regular angels, making it even harder to believe the universe is young! Watchman Nee said, "slain" should be translated, "newly slain," which would show how we can apply the freshness His sacrifice. (COME LORD JESUS, p. 67).

TWELVE

Noah's Flood And All Of The Species On Earth

CAN THE RELATIVELY FEW "KINDS" OF ANIMALS YEC SAYS WERE on Noah's Ark, have produced all of the "species" on Earth now, combined with those that went extinct since the Flood? That's the question I will answer now.

Genetics! Genetics! Genetics! Genetics prove conclusively that all evolutionary theories concerning how animals got here are absolutely impossible.

In their 2002 book, "Acquiring Genomes: A Theory of the Origins of Species," (pp. 11-12), evolutionists Lynn Margulis, (U. Of Mass. Amherst), and Carl Sagon's son Dorion, said although, "many ways to induce mutations are known … none leads to new organs or new tissues … even professional evolutionary biologists are hard put to find mutations, experimentally induced or spontaneous, that lead in a positive way to evolutionary change."

Molecular biologist Soren Lovtrup, of the University of Gothenburg in Sweden, writes, "micromutations do occur, but the theory that these alone can account for evolutionary change is either falsified, or else it is an unfalsifiable, hence metaphysical theory. I suppose that nobody will deny that it is a great misfortune if an entire branch of science has become addicted to a false theory. But this is what has happened in biology … I believe that one day the Darwinian myth will be ranked as the greatest deceit in the history of science. When this happens many people will pose the question: "How did this ever happen?" (Darwinism: The Refutation of a Myth, p. 422).

Referring to what Arthur Wallace taught in *The Origin of Animal Body Plans: A Study in Evolutionary Developmental Biology,* Stephen C. Meyer said, "To create significant changes in the forms of animals requires attention to timing. Mutations in genes late in development of an animal will affect relatively few cells and architectural features. That's because by late in development the basic outlines of the body plan have already been established." (Darwin's Doubt p. 259).

Meyer also spoke about **the impossibility of early changes in the genetic code providing the needed information for evolution to take place.** He said, "Nusslein-Volhard and Wieschaus discovered this problem in experiments performed on fruit flies after their first Nobel Prize-winning efforts. In these later experiments they studied protein molecules that influence the organization of different types of cells early in the process of embryological development. These molecules, called "morphogens," including one called Bicoid, are critical to establishing the fruit fly's head-to-tail axis. They found that when these early-acting, body-plan-affecting molecules are perturbed, development shuts down. When mutations occur in the gene that codes for Bicoid, the resulting embryos die--as they do in all other known cases in which mutations occur early in the regulatory genes that affect body-plan formation.

"There are good functional reasons for this, familiar to us from the logic of other complex systems. If an automaker modifies a car's paint color or seat covers, nothing else needs to be altered for the car to operate, because the normal function of the car does not depend upon these features. But if an engineer changes the length of the piston rods in the car's engine, and does not modify the crankshaft accordingly, the engine won't run. Similarly, animal development is a tightly integrated process in which various proteins and cell structures depend upon each other for their function, and later events depend crucially on earlier events. As a result, one change early in the development of an animal will require a host of other coordinated changes in separate but functionally interrelated developmental processes and entities downstream." (Darwin's Doubt pp. 260, 261).

The point is: No matter how much time is allotted and no matter how many minor changes take place, no animal's basic body plan can ever change. All of its ancestors and offspring will always be basically the same. There are no evolutionary trees. That's true genetics! That's true science! The Apostle Paul told us we should be "Avoiding worldly, empty chatter--the opposing arguments of what is falsely called 'science.'" (I Timothy 6:20). All of the facts prove conclusively that Genesis One had it right when it said every "kind" of animal was "created," never needing to evolve. No "kind" can macro-evolve into a different "species." Nobody can explain the difference between "kind" and "species."

At this point I want to explain what is meant by: "micromutations do occur." It's similar to saying: "microevolution does occur." And in a sense, in microevolution, new "species" are made! In both evolutionist and creationist literature, "evolution" and "species" have two different meanings! It can mean the body-plan remains the same, though they cannot mate, or it may mean the body-plan has changed! The latter has never been observed! When an animal such as the European hornet (Vespa crabro), moves into a new area, it may microevolve into a slightly different European hornet that cannot breed with other European hornets from other nearby or far away places. So these new European hornets are said to be a "new species" even though they are still European hornets and are still called such. For example: there are, "Vespa crabro flavofasciata, Vespa crabro birulai, and Vespa crabro gribodoi, among several others. The three-named "species" are known as "Trinomial nomenclature," (three-part name). Evolution cannot change the basic body plan, neither quickly nor over a long period of time. Just the body colors and/or patterns (paint jobs), change slightly. So although microevolution is known to happen, it is also known that genetics will not allow European hornets to evolve into anything except other European hornets. That's why it's stated above that this type of thing **cannot account for new animals.**

British evolutionary embryologist Gavin de Beer wrote: "Because homology implies community of descent from ... a common ancestor, it might be thought that genetics would provide the key to the problem of homology. This is where the worst shock of all is encountered ... Characters controlled by identical genes are not necessarily homologous ... homologous structures need not be controlled by identical genes. ... It is now clear that the pride with which it was assumed that the inheritance of homologous structures from a common ancestor explained homology was misplaced." (Homolgy: An Unsolved Problem pp. 15-16).

Evolutionist C. P. Martin said, "mutations are really assaults on the organism's central being, its basic capacity to be a living thing." (American Scientist (1953) "A Non-Geneticist Looks at Evolution" p. 102).

American geneticist and Nobel Prize winner Hermann J. Muller said, "the great majority of mutations, certainly well over 99 percent, are harmful in some way, as is to be expected of the effects of accidental occurrences." (1950 American Scientist "Radiation Damage to the Genetic Material" 38:33--50,126, p. 353).

THIRTEEN

Local Creationism And The Statement Of Fact View
(Comparing It With Today's Main Theories)

1) YOUNG EARTH CREATIONISM

SINCE THERE'S NO ACCOUNT OF THE CREATION OF WATER OR angels and no history of Satan's fall; their inserting them into Genesis, makes their scenario less-literal and less-historical. When things as important as water and angels are missing, I contend it's because they were created BEFORE GENESIS. Certainly that makes more sense than to say they were created in the time-of-Genesis, but Moses failed to tell us! Then in order for the Earth to be less than 12,000 years old (and many believe about 6,000), huge volcanism, continental-drift (moving the continents to where they are, when one giant continent split and drifted apart), an Ice-Age, meteorites in sizes and numbers enough to destroy the Earth many-times-over and a water-surge strong enough to carve the Grand Canyon; all happened in conjunction with Noah's Flood?? This despite the fact that those aboard the Ark didn't get seasick?? This makes their account of Noah's Flood less-literal and less-historical! I have found that, "YEC inserts their science to tell Genesis what it should've said!" My point is: "Where Genesis doesn't say something happened, YEC shouldn't add it to prove their point! The reason these huge events aren't in Genesis is because, they happened BEFORE GENESIS!

2) GOD-GUIDED EVOLUTION

Darwin did not see a chain leading from one animal body-plan to another in the fossil record or on Earth in his day! I haven't seen it happening in the wilderness of New York State! Nor have I heard of anyone seeing it anywhere! If this type of evolution happens, or ever happened, why not now??

3) THE GAP THEORY

This was a theory held by many of our best scholars for over 100 years! I was a Gapper for 40+years. Its proposal is that there's a gap-of-unknown-time (most thought billions of years), between Genesis 1:1 and 1:2. "In the beginning God created the heavens and the Earth" (gap), "The earth was formless and void" etc.! The thought was that Lucifer fell in the gap, causing the earth to be wrecked and covered with water and darkness. This theory has fallen out of favor because scholars now know the Hebrew doesn't allow a gap here! So I was also forced to abandon my long-held-belief! As Bruce K. Watlke pointed out above, 1:2, describes the situation in 1:1 and is not sequential, making it impossible for there to be a gap between them. Another problem for Gappers is that "The heavens and the earth," were made at least 9 billion years apart, stretching, I think, the meaning of "beginning" (resheeth), beyond the breaking-point!

4) THE DAY/AGE THEORY

This theory, championed in modern-times by Hugh Ross and his Progressive Creationism, has an impressive following! Hugh is an all-around-scholar! I call him, "Creationists' greatest cosmologist." I have not found anyone as capable of demonstrating, from The Bible and science, that Noah's Flood was local as Ross is! I cannot imagine there's anyone as able to present this theory as well as Hugh! I have learned a lot from this great scientist; but after all of these years, he's never convinced me that the days of Genesis One, are long periods of time! The reasons I don't believe: 1) there's no need for them to be such! There are other ways at arriving at Ross's Universe in The Bible, without equating Genesis 1:1 with the Big Bang, as he's done (Navigating Genesis, pp. 25-28). He thinks "the heavens and the earth" is a Hebrew compound that "refers uniquely to the totality of the physical universe, all its matter, energy, space, and time." If that's true, it means the first verse in The Bible was not understood until more than 3,000 years later; and then only by cosmologists! 2) There is only one evening and one morning in each of the Six Days! 3) There were no animals made on Day Three to pollinate the plants until Day Five. For reasons like this, Hugh doesn't think the Six Days were consecutive! (Navigating Genesis p. 198). 4) Ross claims dinosaurs were created in the-time-of-Genesis, despite the fact that there's no account of their creation or existence (p. 37). This seems strange, since they ruled for 165 million years! I think they were created and ruled BEFORE GENESIS. 5) Adam's creation. There's reason to believe there are a few gaps in Old Testament genealogies, making more than 6,000 years from Adam to now! If 10% are missing, that would put Adam at 6,600 years ago. In his 1994 book, Creation And Time, p. 140, Hugh places "the most reliable … creation of Adam and Eve between about 10,000 and 35,000 years ago (with outside limits at about 6,000 and 60,000 years)." Then in 2014, in his, Navigating Genesis, p. 75, he gave a scenario where, "Noah would have been alive roughly 40,000 years ago and Adam anywhere from 60,000 to 100,000 years ago." If there were at least 20,000 years between Adam and Noah, it's hard to imagine that the human race remained there for a local flood? Has he broken the "law of non-contradiction?" Like with YEC, there's no record of the creation of angels or water--two very important things, that I have created BEFORE GENESIS! Even if we place Adam at 12,000 years ago, it would mean half of our history is missing, Biblically speaking! I think these ancient humans Ross knows of, were created BEFORE GENESIS, and are not descended from Adam and Eve. In the online, "Hunter-Gatherers and the Origins of Religion," Hervey C. Peoples, Pavel Duda and Frank W. Marlowe, said, "Finds at Pinnacle Point in southern Africa (Marean et al. 2007) demonstrate the use and processing of pigment among anatomically modern humans as early as 165,000 years ago (McDougall et al. 2005)." 6) Hugh believes water, the sun, moon, stars, the planet Earth, angels, and the history of Lucifer's good-life and his fall; all happened in the time-of-Genesis, although he does not see an account of any of it in Genesis?? I contend, this all happened BEFORE GENESIS! 7) Hugh believes all of the ultra-huge-events in Earth's-geological-history, happened during the-time-of-Genesis, despite not being mentioned. For example, he believes Ice Ages happened: "Runaway freeze events have covered up to 90 percent of Earth's surface area in an icy blanket." (p.59). Since Genesis tells us of water-movement to reveal dry-land, we'd expect mention of Ice Ages, if they happened during the-time-of-Genesis. Ross believes great-continental-drift happened during the-time-of-Genesis: "All of the movement of land, together and apart, resulted from tectonic forces in Earth's crust." (p.48). Neither of these catastrophes, nor any of the huge meteorite-events, are recorded in Genesis. I believe it's because they occurred BEFORE GENESIS! 8) Ross thinks the, Spirit's "hovering" in 1:2, "hints that God's work of creating life on Earth began very early" and "the geologic record testifies that marine life, in the form of single-celled microorganisms, did indeed arise before all other life forms." (p. 38). The problem is, there's no mention of any type of creation, while God was "hovering" in 1:2. I hope you've noticed that I haven't disputed any of Hugh's science! My only argument has been that the events he interjects into the-time-of-Genesis, are not recorded there because, they occurred BEFORE GENESIS.

FOURTEEN

The Incredible Complexities Of Flight

ERNST MAYR SAID, "IT IS A CONSIDERABLE STRAIN ON ONE'S credulity to assume that finely balanced systems such as certain sense organs (the eye of vertebrates or the bird's feather) could be improved by random mutations." (Systematics and the Origin of Species p. 296, 1942).

Did sight and flight come about without the need of The Bible's infinitely brilliant, powerful and skillful God?

In *Cecil's Storehouse of Human Knowledge,* under the topic: *Is it aerodynamically impossible for bumble bees to fly?,* we find the following (and remember 30,000 generations of fruit fly mutations have shown no progress--only digression). "Their wings work on the same principle as helicopter blades--to be precise, '**reverse-pitch semi-rotary helicopter blades**' to quote one authority. "A moving airfoil, whether it's a helicopter blade or a bee wing, generates a lot more lift than a stationary one. The real challenge with bees wasn't figuring out the aerodynamics but the mechanics: specifically, how bees can move their wings so fast--roughly 200 beats per second, which is 10 or 20 times the firing rate of the nervous system. The trick apparently is that the bee's wing muscles (thorax muscles, actually) don't expand and contract so much as vibrate, like a rubber band. A nerve impulse comes along and twangs the muscle, much as you would a guitar string, and it vibrates the wing up and down a few times until the next impulse comes along."

In **Science unfolds the hidden mechanics of ladybugs wings** (USA Today, 5-14-17) Doyle Rice quoted Kazuya Saito of the University of Tokyo, "The ladybugs' technique for achieving complex folding is quite fascinating and novel, particularly for researchers in the fields of robotics, mechanics, aerospace and mechanical engineering. Beetle wing folding has the potential to change the umbrella design that has been basically unchanged for more than 1,000 years."

In his article: *Hummingbird flight has a clever twist (Tiny birds rotate wrists to generate lift on upstroke) Nature (News) 14 December 2011*, Ed Young said, "Insects do something similar. Smaller animals have to beat their wings faster than larger ones to stay aloft, and they risk losing muscle power in the process. Hummingbirds and insects have converged on the same rotation: by using their muscles efficiently, they can produce a large amount of power with fast but small movements. Most birds produce lift only when they flap their wings downwards, but hummingbirds can do so on the upstroke too by inverting their wings. Insects achieve a similar feat by inverting their wings at the base, but a hummingbird is constrained by its skeleton, so the mechanism for its maneuver has been unknown until now. It's doing this funny thing with its shoulder, flipping the wing back and forth like a fruit fly rather than a pigeon."

In his article: *Why Are Hummingbirds So Stable in Extreme Turbulence? (Texture,* Mar. 12, 2015), Jeff DelViscio said, "Every bird's head remained remarkably stable in the face of up to a 10 mile-an-hour wind, which Sridhar Ravi said he created a "turbulence intensity" of 15%. (Just for comparison, the researchers had experienced pilots try to fly mini-drones in the same tunnel with just 5% turbulence intensity. Not one could keep their craft in the air--much less sucking out of a nectar tube.) What Ravi and colleagues still don't understand is how they do it. It is yet unclear how the hummingbird's brain which is 2.5 times bigger in size compared with those of chickens or turkeys, control the wrist of the animal with such precision and speed in turbulence. But his team is looking in future research at how hummingbirds "recruit" their muscles to fight high winds. As for any hope of us making next generation aircraft--manned or not--based on the hummingbird model, Ravi said that their wings are just too complicated for us to mimic." Were humming birds made by The Bible's infinitely brilliant, powerful and skillful God? In Job's day he knew he was only seeing "The fringes of His wondrous ways." (Job 26:14). Elihu said God is, "Doing great things which we cannot comprehend." (Job 37:5), and "Stand and consider the wonders of God ... The wonders of One perfect in knowledge." (Job 37:14,16).

FIFTEEN

The Wonder Of Sight

NOW LET'S CONSIDER SIGHT! IN *THE ORIGIN OF SPECIES*, DARWIN said, "To suppose that the eye with all its inimitable contrivances for adjusting the focus to different distances, for admitting different amounts of light, and for the correction of spherical and chromatic aberration, could have been formed by natural selection seems, I freely confess, absurd in the highest degree."

Famous evolutionist, Frank Salisbury said, "Even if something as complex as the eye has appeared several times: for example in the squid, the vertebrates, and the arthropods. It's bad enough accounting for the origin of such things once, but the thought of producing them several times according to the modern synthetic theory makes my head swim." (Doubts About the Modern Synthetic Theory of Evolution, p. 338).

We will now pull some nuggets from Carl Zimmer's: **The Scallop Sees With Hundreds of Space-Age Eyes** (NY Times 12-5-17). "Each eye contains a miniature mirror made up of millions of square tiles." "The mirror reflects incoming light onto two retinas, each of which can detect different parts of the scallop's surroundings." "The new research suggests that scallop eyes are more akin to another kind of technology: a reflector telescope of the sort first invented by Newton." Scallop eyes are "weirdly" and "exquisitely complex," with "hidden sophistication" and "Star Wars vision technology." Scallops live in a shell like clams: "Each individual eye sits at the tip of its own tentacle and can extend beyond the rim of the shell." "Benjamin A. Palmer, a postdoctoral researcher at the Weizmann Institute of Science in Israel, and his colleagues recently used a powerful new tool known as a cryo-electron microscope to look at scallop eyes." (see the journal **Science** 11-30-17).

Michael Denton said, "It is the sheer universality of perfection, the fact that everywhere we look, to whatever depth we look, we find an elegance and ingenuity of an absolutely transcending quality, that so mitigates against the idea of chance." (Evolution: A Theory in Crisis, p. 324).

Barney T. Maddox, M. D., said, "Now the genetic difference between human and his [supposed] 'nearest relative,' the chimpanzee, is at least 1.6 percent. That doesn't sound like much, but calculated out, that is a gap of at least 48 million nucleotide differences that must be bridged by random changes. A random change of only three nucleotides is fatal to an animal (and of course, the death of a crippled mutant animal ends all possibility of further change). (*Human Genome Project: Quantitative Disproof of Evolution*, 1992, pp. 1-2).

EVOLUTIONISTS ADMIT THERE'S NOTHING THEY "KNOW" ABOUT EVOLUTION

Evolution has no way to explain anything, let alone why "**ONLY HUMANS WORSHIP.**"

Lewis Thomas said, "Our most spectacular biological attribute, which identifies us as our particular sort of animal, is language, and the deep nature of this gift is a mystery." ("On the Uncertainty of Science," *Key Reporter,* vol. 46, Autumn 1980, p. 1).

On page two Thomas said, "Biology needs a better word than *error* for the driving force in evolution … I cannot make my peace with the randomness doctrine: I cannot abide the notion of purposelessness and blind chance in nature. And yet I do not know what to put in its place for the quieting of my mind."

Darwin said, "If it could be demonstrated that any complex organ existed which could not possibly have been formed by numerous, successive, slight modifications, my theory would absolutely break down." (*The Origin of Species*, 6th *ed., London: John Murray, 1859, p. 182*).

Evolutionist turned creationist, Carl E. Baugh, in *Why do men Believe EVOLUTION Against All Odds?* (p. 80), conveyed, "In 1980 the University of Chicago hosted a conference of the world's leading evolutionary theorists. The conference was entitled "Macroevolution," and their task was to consider the mechanisms that underlie the origin of species. The central question of the Chicago conference was whether the mechanisms underlying *microevolution* can be extrapolated to explain the phenomena of *macroevolution* ... the answer can be given as a clear, **No.**" (Lewin, *Science* Vol. 210, pp. 883-87).

Baugh added (p. 81), "Wolfgang Smith held faculty positions at Oregon State, MIT, and UCLA. His considered opinion is expressed rather forcefully: "{Macroevolution] is **totally bereft of scientific sanction** ... [T]here exists to this day **not a shred of evidence** in support of the thesis that macroevolutionary transformations ever occurred [emphasis Baugh's]." (*Teildardism and the New Religion*, 1988, pp. 5-6).

Darwin said, "Geology assuredly does not reveal any such finely graduated organic chain; and this, perhaps, is the most obvious and gravest objection which can be urged against my theory." (*The Origin of Species by Means of Natural Selection*, first edition reprint, New York: Avenel Books, 1979, p. 292).

Darwin also wondered, "Why, if species have descended from other species by fine gradations, do we not everywhere see innumerable transitional forms? Why is not all nature in confusion, instead of the species being, as we see them, well defined?" (from a chapter in "The Origin of Species" entitled, "Difficulties on Theory").

Note here that Darwin speaks of "species," giving it the

same meaning given by modern scientists when they speak of "macroevolution," which requires a new body-plan, which has never been documented. Whereas "microevelution," is considered to have happened, if the new "species" cannot mate with the animals they "evolved" from. Therefore, whenever you see the word, "species," you must determine whether or not it refers to an animal with a totally different body plan, which has never been seen, or with animals having the same body-plan, but are unable to mate and often are "painted" with a different coloration and/or pattern. So there are two different meanings for "species" and "evolution."

Why don't we see trillions of transitional forms in various stages of becoming a new species of animal? I don't see any when I walk out in nature!

Stephen C. Meyer said, "The Chengjiang fauna makes the Cambrian explosion more difficult to reconcile with Darwinian view for yet another reason. The Chengjiang discoveries intensify the top-down pattern of appearance in which individual representatives of the higher taxonomic categories (phyla, subphyla, and classes) appear and only later diversify into the lower taxonomic categories (families, genera, and species). Discoveries at Chengjiang contradict the bottom-up pattern that neo-Darwinism expects. The site does not show the gradual emergence of unique species followed slowly but surely by the emergence of representatives of ever higher and more disparate taxa, leading novel phyla. Instead, like the Burgess Shale, it shows body plan-level disparity arising first and suddenly, with no evidence of a gradual unfolding and ranging through the lower taxonomic groups." (*Darwin's Doubt p. 74*).

All of this means that **"slow, gradual (microevolution), never can produce new body forms"** and **"quick-large-change (macroevolution) is impossible." Both are genetically impossible.** In other words, **"All animals must only have ancestors like themselves, going back to when God created them." Genesis 1:20-25 tells us God made every "kind" of animal complete, with no ability or need to evolve into** another "kind." And since macroevolution cannot happen, "kind" and "species" are the same.

In his 2010 article: **No Fruit Fly Evolution Even After 600 Generations,** Brian Thomas, M. S. (Institute for Creation Research), said, "If evolutionary biologists could document such evolution in action, they could vindicate their worldview and cite real research to support their surreal claims. In 1980, this search for proof led researchers to painstakingly and purposefully mutate each core gene involved in the fruit fly development. The now classic work, for which the authors won the Nobel Prize in 1995, was published in *Nature*. The experiments proved that the mutation of any of these core developmental genes--mutations that would be essential for the fruit fly to evolve into any other creature--merely resulted in dead or deformed fruit flies. This therefore showed that fruit flies could not evolve. Similarly, Michigan State University evolutionary biologist Richard Lenski and his colleagues searched for signs of evolution in bacteria for 20 years, tracking 40,000 generations. In the end, the species that they started with was hobbled by accumulated mutations, and the only changes that had occurred were degenerative. University of Bristol emeritus professor of bacteriology Alan Linton summarized the situation:

'But where is the experimental evidence? None exists in the literature claiming that one species has been shown to evolve into another. Bacteria, the simplest form of independent life, are ideal for this kind of study, with generation times of 20 to 30 minutes, and populations achieved after 18 hours. But throughout 150 years of the science of bacteriology, there is no evidence that one species of bacteria has changed into another, in spite of the fact that populations have been exposed to potent chemical and physical mutagens and that, uniquely, bacteria possess extra-chromosomal, transmissible plasmids. Since there is no evidence for species changes between the simplest forms of unicellular life, it is not surprising that there is no evidence for evolution from prokaryotic to eukaryotic cells, let alone throughout the whole array of higher multicellular organisms.'"

Natural Selection, Chance and Randomness are meaningless terms. We can never expect anything that has the look of brilliance to come from them. They are all powerless, brainless, deaf, sightless, purposeless and thoughtless; unable to plan or conceive a blueprint. They have no knowledge. They are nothing! The field I've become something of an expert in, concerns social wasps (like yellowjackets), and social bees (like honey bees and bumble bees). I've had the great pleasure of drawing from the vast knowledge of world-renowned experts: Robbin W. Thorp (bumble bees), John W. Wenzel (wasps), and Thomas D. Seeley (honey bees). Just because I disagreed with them concerning how these insects got here (they are evolutionists), I did not hesitate relying on them for deep insight into the things these bees and wasps can do and how they do them, now that they're here.

What do top evolutionists mean when they say they do not KNOW anything about evolution? Simply this: "There's no evolutionary question they can answer with certainty. There's nothing they can prove. There's nothing they KNOW. I have asked my evolutionary-entomologist friends a few questions concerning evolution and they did not KNOW the answer to any. The BEST they ever could do was guess. "But many times they couldn't even do that. I have come to realize that these entomologists' high-intelligence and awesome-knowledge often works against them because, their expertise enables them to make enough sense out of non-sense to convince themselves and others that the impossible most assuredly is true. They can spin the story in such a way that the general public is not aware that the entire narrative is based on guesses--not science. But when pressed, they must admit that they made it up and they do not KNOW what happened. Everything is based on ASSUMTIONS--not knowledge. The famous skeptic, Michael Shermer, said, "Smarter people are better at rationalizing bad ideas."

Let's look at a small sample of the questions that caused the evolutionists above to admit that they "Do not know a single thing about evolution."

I asked my evolutionist/entomologist friends. "Is there any insect whose direct ancestor is known?" Everyone told me, "No!" James M. Carpenter of the Museum of Natural History in NYC, said, "No is certainly the answer to that question." If any theory of evolution were true, we should see at least trillions of examples of this, both in the fossil record and happening now. How can it be that none of these are **KNOWN?** It certainly points overwhelmingly to the fact that no animal has ever had ancestors or offspring other than those with the same body-plan, just as genetics and The Bible have taught us.

On page 125 of **CHANCE AND THE SOVEREIGNTY OF GOD,** Vern S. Poythress said, "In this kind of context, "chance" appears to be moving toward being a substitute god. It is chance with a capital C. A blank space in our knowledge now becomes a positive explanation. It is religiously motivated by the need for a substitute for God. The word *chance* appears to do the job until we ask whether we know what it is. It is simply what we do not know! Chance is somewhat of an embarrassment to evolutionary naturalism, because as a philosophy naturalism aspires to give a rational, humanly intelligible explanation of life. Its approach is a form of rationalism, because it wants to exercise reason independent of God. But at the heart of the explanation is Chance, which is irrational. Moreover, what is left as irrational is a potential source of divine action. Every instance of "chance," according to a theistic point of view, is an instance of divine control, and so injects purpose into the cosmos, even though philosophical naturalism must dogmatically assert that the events are without purpose."

Eric F. Wieschaus, of the famed fruit fly mutation study, told the audience at a 1982 American Association for the Advancement of Science, "The problem is, we think we've hit all the genes required to specify the body plan of *Drosophila*, and yet these results are obviously not promising as raw materials for macroevolution. The next question then, I guess, is what *are*--or what *would be* --the right mutations for major evolutionary change? And we don't know the answer to that."

The most difficult insect to explain through evolutionary processes is the honey bee. Honey bees are so unlike any other insect and can do so many highly-complicated things that nobody can even begin to give us a rational explanation, according to knowledge, concerning how they "evolved." What makes their existence so particularly difficult to explain, is that they always needed to be able to do many extremely complex things in an amazingly precise way. If there was even one, of many things, they couldn't do, they could not exist.

Honey bees propagate through an ultra-complicated process known as "swarming." It's a trillion times easier to send a rover to explore Mars than it is to program honey bees so that they'll be able to swarm! Yet to exist they must know when and how to do this. No evolutionist has the slightest clue as to how they were able to propagate "before" they "evolved" the ability to swarm. Yet if evolution is true, they had to have had some method. That's a moot point anyway because, evolutionists don't KNOW how honey bees got here in the first place? They cannot point to a single piece of "knowledge" concerning how they came to exist!

Let's look at the basics of swarming. At a certain time of year (usually May/June in NYS), about 11,000 workers "decide" to leave the hive and coax the queen to come with them. They must "know" the many different things they must do to successfully establish a new colony. My entomologist friends all assure me that these insects cannot reason. As I always say, "Somebody reasoned!" They "know" how to do everything and when to do it. For example, before leaving the hive, they know they must gorge on honey in order to keep them alive during the swarming process--this stomach-full of honey gives them 7 days to find a new place to live. They "know" they must feed the queen less than usual so she'll be able to fly. They "know" they must land somewhere (usually on a limb), forming a "swarm cluster." From there, about 400 special scouts "know" they must go out from the cluster surface in search for a new place to live. Then in an almost unbelievable give-and-take, they "discuss" where they should build their new hive, almost always agreeing on one of the best places available for miles around. One question is: "If evolution was true why would the bees swarm in the first place, since it wouldn't do any good until they "learned" how to find and move into a new home?" For the astonishing details about swarming, see Thomas D. Seeley's, "Honeybee Democracy."

In the meanwhile, back at the original hive, the bees there also must "know" what to do in order to survive now that their queen has left. Well-before the swarm left, the bees "knew" they had to build several extra-large, peanut-shell-looking-cells hanging down from the combs. The old queen "knew" she had to lay an egg in each. The bees "knew" they had to feed these larvae an extra-nutritious substance called, "royal jelly." The large cells and the royal jelly produce new queens. The first one to emerge "knows" she must sting all the unborn queens to death. If more than one emerges at once, they fight to the death and the last queen standing rules the colony.

The new queens in a given area "know" they must fly out from the hive. The new, recently born males also fly away. These new queens and males have never been anywhere in their lives, yet in some ultra-mysterious way they will go to a "drone congregation area" that may be three miles away. These areas are about 60 feet high and may be above a lake, a field, woods and/or a mountain. Science cannot explain their existence, much less how the males and queens are finding them. Honey bees are not native to North America, yet when they got here these male congregation areas were waiting for them? Incredibly, year after year the new males and queens, "know" how to find these same places. Since the bees from several hives from up to a few miles around go there, each queen mates with about 10 males, giving her possible one million offspring, good health-producing genetic diversity.

Astonishingly, swarming and the things associated with it are among honey bees' least complicated abilities. The ability of 60,000+

honey bees in a colony to operate as a cohesive unit is an example of something far more unlikely to ever be explained. Scientists sometimes act as though by describing something, they've solved the mystery! This causes me to bring up a famous scientific-mantra, I hope you'll never forget! Knowing it can prevent scientists from pulling-a-fast-one on you! Here it is: "JUST BECAUSE YOU'VE DESCRIBED SOMETHING, DOESN'T MEAN YOU'VE EXPLAINED IT!" Honey bees in a given colony are all somehow able to "know" what their task should be at a given time. Some get water, some get nectar, some feed the larvae, some feed the queen, some fan the hive with their wings to keep it cool enough, some are undertakers that remove dead bees to prevent disease, some guard the entrance and some dance to tell others where a good flower source is. At any given time, there is a baffling efficiency! How can we explain this? The late Cambridge professor, Ludwig Wittgenstein, wrote, "The great delusion of modernity is that the laws of nature explain the universe for us. The laws of nature describe the universe, they describe the regularities. But they explain nothing." (from his online quotes).

Honey bees' ability to make honey (the eternal food), certainly cannot be explained apart from an infinitely intelligent and skillful God. Do you think blind unintelligent forces programmed honey bees with the ability to make honey that was still good, though thousands of years old in an Egyptian tomb? Did their ability to make such a sweet and nourishing substance come about by chance? When John the Baptist lived in the wilderness "his diet was locusts and wild honey" (Mark 1:6). I must say a better diet than most of us have!

Then without a compass or ruler, honey bees make perfect and uniform hexagon cells. How can it be that they able to do this? How is it that it is that these primitive little insects, with a brain the size of two grains of sand, "know" how to build honeycombs; the most efficiently-designed-structure possible for storing honey, since each of a cell's six sides is also the side of a cell next to it. Not only is it optimal in the use of space, but it is also extremely strong, which is why the "honeycomb" design is used in airplane wings and in rocket ship walls. The bees build these honeycombs vertically, with the horizontal cells slightly tilted upward so they can cap them from the bottom up, without honey leaking out. They are able to make these perfect cells in the darkness of the hive by reading the Earth's magnetic field. When a large magnet is placed over the hive, the bees make botched and inefficient cells.

Honeycombs are made out of an amazing wax that comes into being in an incredible way. One of the ways honey bees are able to continue to get all the jobs done in the colony at any given time is because, they do a certain job at a certain age. When the summer worker honey bees turn about 10 days old (they live about 35 days), they develop wax-producing glands in their abdomens, from which they secrete wax for about a week. This wax dries hard and strong, becoming ideal for making honeycombs. Evolutionists want us to believe that honey bees and all of their knowledge and abilities exist without being created by a God with infinite knowledge, power and skill. The early apostles had to confront such people and that's why the Apostle Paul asked, "Where is the scholar? Where is the scribe? Where is the debater of this age? Has not God made foolish the wisdom of this world?" (I Corinthians 1:20). Job said, "These are but the fringes of His wonders."

From early September through early December, the queen lays eggs that turn into "winter bees." Warm weather bees only live about 35 days, whereas winter bees can live up to six months. In this way there are plenty of workers there to feed the several thousand new workers needed in the spring. When we look in on a honey bee colony, we are gazing at and comprehending something of God's "Divine nature and eternal power" (Romans 1:20). There's no other logical explanation! Much of what the bees know and how they "learned" is unknown and unknowable. God does things past finding out. Everyone should be able to realize there must be a God. But The Bible knows that not everyone "sees." And why don't they "see?" Jesus told of people who, "Having eyes, they see not." Of others He said, "Their eyes have they closed." Still others "Satan has blinded the minds of those who do not believe." Jesus knew of those, "Who always resist the Truth." He spoke of people who wouldn't believe even if, "one came back from the dead." Let's try an experiment! There's nothing to lose! Fall on your knees (even if you're an atheist), and pray, "Oh God, if You're there and listening, please reveal Yourself to me." If you cannot do that, it shows you have a closed mind with no desire at all to know the Truth. You cannot come to God with your PHD or any other form of greatness or pride! No! No! No! You must humble yourself like a child! (Matthew 18:2-4).

THE BOOK OF NATURE

The Bible teaches us about God and so does **The Book of Nature.** I think that written within nature, God has revealed four major things about Himself. 1. He is not boring. 2. He does whatever pleases Him. 3. He loves us. 4. He is a Holy God Who hates sin. The fact that any animal has to die, teaches us that, despite God's great love for His creation, He must show us how much He hates sin. Jesus said, "Are not five sparrows sold for two cents? Yet not one of them is forgotten before God. Indeed, the very hairs of your head are numbered." (Not only does God know how many hairs are on each head! He knows the sequential number of each hair!) "Do not fear; you are more valuable than many sparrows." (Luke 12:6-7).

WHY WE CAN TRUST THE BIBLE AS
THE WRITTEN WORD OF GOD

There has never been a Book like The Bible! It's by far the most read, most loved and most hated book ever written anywhere in the universe! The devil and his minions are out in full-force attempting to diminish, debunk and destroy it. In Satan-run places like China, it's against the law to own a Bible. Watchman Nee, spent the last 17 years of his life in prison there for preaching from The Bible. There are Christians who, at great risk, spend their lives smuggling Bibles into China. God's Word cannot be stopped! The Bible is a spiritual Book, that cannot be fully understood as it should be by the unaided human mind (1 Cor. 2:14). Although it's a book of spiritual facts, at the same time it teaches us science, history and prophecy (history written in advance). In the following quote from the 1910 book, *The Interpreting Bible*, William Blackwood (D.D., L.L.D.), shows us why we can rely on The Bible.

PRESERVATION.--The Sacred Scriptures are not only genuine and authentic, but they have been transmitted to us uncorrupted and unmutilated. That they have come down to us--in all essential points--the same as they were given by the authors, rests on most satisfactory evidence. A few letters or even unimportant words may have been omitted or changed in the lapse of ages by transcribers, but the fact is established that the Holy Scriptures have suffered less from the injury of time than any other ancient writings whatever. Even the most imperfect manuscripts extant would not change an article of our faith or ignore one moral precept.

The original manuscripts of the Old Testament were preserved with the utmost care by the Jews, who were famed for their faithful guardianship of their Sacred Books. Even the words and letters were enumerated, and a constant watchfulness was maintained lest errors or omissions should prevail. The translation of the Old Testament into the Septuagint Version when the Canon was closed, the spread of the Jews into different lands with manuscripts in their possession, the division of the Jews into sects and parties who watched each other with jealousy. Clearly show that before the time of Christ fabrication or omission was impossible. After that event, the Christians exercised as watchful a care over these books as the Jews had done, and any attempt at fraud by Jews or Christians would immediately have been detected and exposed.

The integrity and purity of the New Testament are equally

unquestionable. The rapid multiplication of early manuscripts and translations into other tongues, the spread of copies into distant lands, the reverence of the Christians for their Sacred Books, the rise of sects and parties who generally appealed to the same authority for the truth of their respective systems, unite in showing that any material alteration in these books could not have been made without the fact being known; and thus the ever-watchful hand of Providence may be clearly seen in the manner in which the Sacred Text has been preserved from century to century through the most troubled periods. The histories of mighty empires and treatises on philosophy and literature of great value have perished, and can never be recovered; but the Sacred Scriptures, though more ancient and exposed to the savage hostility of men who sought their destruction by every means, have been faithfully preserved. The prophets never accused the Jews of falsifying their Sacred Books. Jesus charged the Jews with unbelief and other grrievous sins, but never with the guilt of mutilating or destroying any part of the Old Testament. An examination of nearly twelve hundred manuscripts afford a remarkable proof of uncorrupted preservation and identity. All other books have shared the usual fate of the progress of time. They have been worn out, neglected or destroyed; but the loving care, the watchful jealousy and honest guardianship which have ever been displayed in the preservation of the Sacred Books, even to the numbering of the words and the letters, are without a parallel, and thus we have secured to us the pure and uncorrupted revelation of God's holy will."

SIXTEEN

The Bible's God And His Incredibly Accurate Prophecies

ONE OF THE REASONS SKEPTICS HATE THE BIBLE, IS BECAUSE OF ITS undeniably amazing, accurate predictions. **Bible prophecy is: "history written in advance,"** and cannot possibly ever be wrong. If someone uses Bible and makes a prediction that fails, it only means they interpreted the prophecy incorrectly because they didn't know what to look for. Unfortunately, such has been the case several times concerning Christ's second coming, giving skeptics false hope that it will never happen. These Christians usually had what seemed to be valid reasons for their beliefs. Their hearts were in the right place! They longed for His return and were right to do so. They made honest mistakes. After Jesus failed to appear on New Years in 2000, skeptics had their day in the sun. They foolishly derided those who expected His return. Here is a sample from the SKEPTICAL INQUIRER Vol. 24.1 January/February 2000. In his article "Notes of a Fringe Watcher: The Second Coming of Jesus," Matin Gardner, showed his blindness by ignorantly saying:

"You would think that believers in the imminence of Christ's return would be bothered by the fact that, **ever since the** gospels were written, huge numbers of Christians have interpreted Biblical signs of the end as applying to *their* generation. The sad history of these failed prophecies makes no impression on the mind-sets of today's fundamentalists. Even Billy Graham, who should've known better, has for decades preached and written about the impending return of Jesus. He grants that no one knows the exact year, but all signs indicate, he believes, that the great event is almost upon us."

Oh wow! Well, first of all I'd like to thank Gardner and all like him for helping to fulfill Peter's prophecy concerning these last days! "Know this first of all, That in the last days mockers will come mocking, following their own desires, and saying, 'Where is the promise of His coming? For **since the** fathers fell asleep, all continues just as it was from the beginning of creation.' For when they maintain this, **it escapes their notice** that by the Word of God heavens existed long ago … But do not let this one escape your notice, beloved, that with the Lord one day is like a thousand years, and a thousand years like one day." (II Peter 3:3-5,8). Why was this so important to Peter? We will explore that and much more below. Let me say here that Adam and Eve weren't said to have existed "long ago," as the heavens are here! This subject of the end-times is a perfect example of how "skeptics"minds make it impossible for them to analyze the facts with an open-mind. Even when they are shown clear obvious facts, they cannot "see" them. No clear-thinking open-minded-person, when shown the facts, will doubt that we're in the end-times. There are so many prophecies that appeared extremely unlikely, but are now happening, that the conclusion we're in the last days is unavoidable!

Secondly, this Biblically-ignorant "skeptic" thinks he knows more about the whether we're in end-times or not than Billy Graham did?!? Billy thought Jesus was coming back soon! Can he be wrong? Absolutely not! There's a zero percent chance that Jesus will wait much longer! If there's one thing everyone should know about modern so-called, self-proclaimed "skeptics," it's that they are not skeptics at all. They are atheists and evolutionists who hate The Bible's God, which explains why Peter said that creation by The Word of God, **"escapes their notice."** They are modern Saducees! They have "unbelieving-brains" that do not allow them to accept anything that scares or upsets them. They cannot let anything exist that challenges their narrow little world-view. They are never skeptical of evolutionary theories, atheism or their other cockeyed-ideas! They are the greatest case ever seen of, "A little knowledge is dangerous!" When "skeptics" study weird and scary subjects like prophecy or the paranormal, their conclusions are ALWAYS predetermined and ALWAYS go against the world's leading experts. Their brains are hard-wired to say, "Nothing strange is happening!" They have NEVER researched deeply. Whether it is haunted houses, UFOs, angels helping people, bigfoot-type creatures, ghosts, crop circles, or Bible Prophecy, they do a cursory research and consider themselves as experts who are superior to those who've devoted their entire lives (many times over 40 years), to studying one or more of these subjects. That "skeptics" NEVER know what they're talking about concerning these scary subjects is easily shown by comparing what is being said by the world's top experts and the small portion of it that these "skeptics," "debunk." They don't even cover many well-known (among the experts), aspects of the subjects they address. They NEVER do a comprehensive study on any of these subjects because, the truth, no doubt, terrifies them too much to really find out what's going on. They NEVER explain the facts, they **explain them away.** Yet, I get the impression that they are not lying or purposely deceiving us. They actually convince themselves into believing utter absurdities like: "The end-times are not here." It's also obvious that they're intelligent, for as Michael Shermer points out, "It takes intelligence to make absurdities look like truth."

The Sadducees said, "there is no resurrection, nor an angel nor a spirit" (Acts 23:8), so they were "Sad-you-see." Now, you will never forget who the Sadducees were, no matter how hard you try!

I understand why skeptics feel as they do. I know we've cried, "Wolf!" enough in the past to cause them to scoff at any new predictions. But though the entire "Skeptical Inquirer" article appears to be "intellectual," with "legitimate complaints," yet it is deeply flawed, being written from the standpoint of ignorance. The author knows so little about the universe's all-time (by far), greatest-selling book (The Bible, over 5 billion copies), that he cannot even state how believers arrived at their predictions. So I will help him and at the same time explain why, "The sad history of these failed prophecies makes no impression on the mind-sets of today's fundamentalists." First of all, there was not and has never been a "failed Bible prophecy," only misunderstood timing by prognosticators.

What these "skeptics" fail to understand, in their overwhelming ignorance, is that **things are different now--far different!** They are so blind that **TRUTH** makes no impression on them, just like Noah's preaching made no impression on those who were swept away in the Flood. Billy Graham knew we were in the end-times and we lesser Christian know it. We are not guessing--we know it this time!

Why do fundamentalists, despite past misses, still again, think we're in the last days? I know that sounds arrogant, but it's the truth. Both the Scriptural-timing and the signs-of-the-times, tell us with certainty! And why are we so sure? It's easy to see that the last days are upon us by looking at what's going on in the world! But I have the feeling that "skeptics," no matter how spectacular the signs are, will refuse to believe until it's too late. They will simply attribute everything to "coincidence." No matter how silly it is to do so, "skeptics" will insist it's all just a series of "coincidences." Skeptics never get tired of saying, "coincidence." They think the world is operating according to "Time and Chance" (Ecclesiastes 9:11).

The FACT is, those who mistakenly thought Jesus was coming back when He didn't return, are still far closer to the truth than those who don't think He's coming back anytime soon or don't think He's coming back at all.

BIBLE PROPHECY IS HISTORY WRITTEN IN ADVANCE

Christians have known and now know the future, in ways unknown the the rest of the world. Over a hundred years ago we predicted a

One-World-Government would be here at the end and now it is clearly in view for everyone to see. We predicted many Jews would return to Israel and reestablish it as a nation, which happened in 1948, an event so extremely unlikely without God, it was unforeseen by the secular world. We predicted Global Jihad, while the secular world slept without seeing it coming! In 1995 Victor Mordecai wrote the book, "Is Fanatic Islam A Global Threat?" The secular world thinks things will go on and on as usual. But super-drastic-changes are, obviously to Christians, almost here.

1. **BIBLE PROPHECY** All Bible prophecies that were supposed to happen in the past, were fulfilled, even though many seemed impossible. For example, despite being the furthest thing from Jewish thought, the Old Testament predicted their Great King and Messiah would suffer immensely and die on a tree. It said He'd be born in Bethlehem and yet somehow be "called out of Egypt." Harold Hoehner, proved that Daniel's 69 sevens (483 years of 360 days each) "until Messiah," only needed one cloudy day (which was probable since it was already within one day), in order to bring us to the day of Messiah's triumphal entry into Jerusalem in the spring of 33 AD, exactly 483 years later, as Daniel predicted.

2. **THE JEWS** When asked, "What is the best proof that The Bible is The Word of God?," the overwhelming consensus of scholars is: "The Jews." Probably the all-time hardest-to-explain prophecy ever, concerns the Jews being scattered to the four winds for over 1,800 years, remaining a people, and being brought back to their homeland where once again, "The desert will shout for joy and blossom like the crocus."(Isaiah 35:1). Yahweh said, "I will bring them back and they will live in the midst of Jerusalem." (Zechariah 8:8). Jesus said, when the fig tree "grows its leaves, you know summer is near. So you too, when you see all theses things, recognize that He is near; at

the door. Truly I say to you, this generation will not pass away until all these things take place." (Matthew 24:32). One of "these things" Jesus was talking about being here before "this generation" passes away, was, "the Holy place." (Matt. 24:15), in the Jewish Temple.

3. **THE JEWISH TEMPLE WILL SOON (I THINK BEFORE 2030) BE REBUILT ON THE TEMPLE MOUNT IN JERUSALEM.** I suppose this prophecy's fulfillment may be even harder to imagine than #2 above, because it's even more specific. End-time Bible prophecies cannot come true unless the Temple is built within the next few years. Humanly speaking, it's an impossibility! But Jesus said, "The things that are impossible with people are possible with God." (Luke 18: 27). Some of the incredibly unlikely factors have already been taken care of, with others being in the process. The number of seemingly impossible jobs and determinations that must be accomplished in order for the Temple to be built exactly as it was and where it was, so the sacrifices could be re-initiated, is truly mind-boggling! More so even than any of us could have guessed. The huge, skillfully made holy alter, has already been built. The Temple's sacred attire and artifacts have been skillfully made. The blue dye made from rare ocean snails, the only dye (blue) allowed in the priest's robe, has been made. **But the biggest, seemingly unsolvable problem, is the fact that the Temple with everything in it, must be built exactly where it use to be on the Temple Mount And the top scholars all know it will be constructed precisely where the "Dome of the Rock" now resides. The "Dome of the Rock" will soon be torn down and removed.** So with hundreds of millions of Muslims having the attitude, "I'll die first," how can this happen? How can this prophecy ever come true? As always, it's easy for The Bible's God to make prophecy happen.

In order to find out how the Temple can be built in the only permissible place, we must look to other prophecies. Jesus said, "Elijah is coming and he will restore all things." (Matt. 17: 11). This is the answer! Elijah and Enoch (to help him), are God's two witnesses, being the only two people taken to heaven alive. But what about all of Israel's Jew-hating neighbors? Are they going to stand by and allow this to happen? These two witnesses are not to be messed with! God said, "I will grant authority to my two witnesses, and they will prophesy for twelve hundred and sixty days, clothed in sackcloth. These are the two olive trees and the two lampstands that stand before the Lord of all the Earth. And if anyone wants to harm them, fire flows out of their mouths and devours their enemies. So if anyone desires to harm them, he must be killed in this way. These have the power to shut up the sky, so that rain will not fall during the days of their prophesying; and they have power over the waters to turn them into blood, and to strike the Earth with every plague, as often as they desire." (Revelation 11: 3-6). Anyone who resists their tearing down the Dome of the Rock and the building of the Jewish Temple will be hit with either instant death or a plague from Enoch's and Elijah's mouths.

The Bible plainly tells us what will happen during these final days of this Age. To make predictions is extremely easy. There are some of you who are thinking, "If I see these two prophets, watching over the building of the Temple and killing people who oppose them with fire coming out of their mouths (or if fire is a metaphor, they will yell at them or breath on them), then I will believe and turn to God." The problem with that is: **Time is not on your side!** "Now is the acceptable time...now is the day of salvation" (2 Cor. 6:2). You are not guaranteed another day! Billy Graham left us with these final words: "God loves you and you have very little time!"

What must you do? You say, "I don't 'feel' or 'sense' God's love for me. What should I do? Time is fast running out! What should I do? I stand on the brink of eternity! What should I do? Before me lies my destiny: Eternal Paradise or the Eternal Lake of Fire! What should I do?"

Solomon said, "The fear of the Lord is the beginning of wisdom, and the knowledge of the Holy One is understanding" (Proverbs 9:10). "Perfect love casts out fear." (1 John 4:18) Seek Him with all of your heart. Humble yourself in His presence. Life is certainly a mystery! But one thing we know, we cannot save ourselves! If God doesn't forgive us for our sins, we are doomed to pay for them ourselves for eternity. Oh but you say, "I'm not such a bad sinner." Don't be blind like the pharisee (religious leader), who prayed by an evil tax-collector. Luke 18:9-14 says, "And He (Jesus), told this parable (a story that does happen), to some people who trusted in themselves that they were righteous, and viewed others with contempt: "Two men went up into the temple to pray, one a Pharisee and te other a tax-collector. The Pharisee stood and was praying this to himself: 'God I thank You that I am not like other people: swindlers, unjust, adulterers, or even like this tax collector. I fast twice a week: I pay tithes of all I get' But the tax-collector, standing some distance away, was unwilling to even lift up his eyes to heaven, but was beating his chest, saying, 'God be merciful to me a sinner' I tell you this man went to his house justified rather than the other; for everyone who exalts himself will be humbled, but he who humbles himself will be exalted." The Pharisee was in darkness, needing God's light as we all do. The tax-collector, knowing he cheated people by skimming money off the top, knew he was a sinner, needing forgiveness!

THE BIBLE PREDICTED MUSLIMS
WOULD BE HERE AT THE END

There are several prophetic statements that show The Bible knew Muslims would be here. I have some Muslim friends and God hasn't withheld salvation from anyone who truly seeks Him with all of their heart. (Jeremiah 29:13). Many Muslims in the past few years, have given their hearts to Jesus. Some have seen the actions of other Muslims and realized they were killing non-Muslims in accordance with the Quran. Others have had Jesus come to them in a dream. I believe many more will realize Jesus is the Son of God, and will turn to Him when they see the deadly-accuracy of Bible prophecy. From what I'm reading, more Muslims are turning to Christ than any other grouping! Even though they seek the wrong God, the true God honors those who seek with all their hearts and Jesus reveals Himself to them, and many become born again Christians! Nevertheless, in God's plan, Muslims will kill millions of Christians and Jews! So in what ways does The Bible tell us Muslims will be here in these last days? Remember this: Jesus knows which Muslims will eventually love and serve Him. He defends Israel, so the nations will know he's God. Ezekiel 39:7 says, "My holy name I will make known in the midst of My people Israel; and I will not let My holy name be profaned anymore. And the nations will know that I Am Yahweh, the Holy One of Israel."

1. Jesus said, "the hour is coming when whoever kills you will think they're serving God." (John 16:2). The Quran in Surah 9:5 says, "Then kill disbelievers (non-Muslims) wherever you find them." Of course not all Muslims obey, but enough do!

2. Their Mahdi, the Bible's Antichrist, will be on the Temple Mount to make a treaty that will halt Enoch and Elijah from killing the Muslim world. Muslims are not the only ones who will hold this person in high-regard. I think he is already a well-known, well-liked figure on the world-stage. I don't think he's someone who comes out of left-field! Without the Muslims and their Dome of the Rock, there would be no need for Elijah, with the help of his friend Enoch, to return to "restore all things" by killing those who oppose them with 'fire flowing out of their mouths" and there would be no need for Antichrist to make a treaty with the Jews. (Matt. 17:11, Rev. 11:4-5, Dan.9:27). At precisely 2,520 days before Jesus returns

to Earth, Enoch and Elijah will return to the Temple Mount and begin to kill Muslims with fire out of their mouths, so the Dome of the Rock can be torn down and the Jewish Temple can be built in its place. On the same day, Antichrist will see this and realize he must tell the Muslims to stop or they'll come in from nations all around and be killed. As much as the Muslims love their precious Dome of the Rock (built where they think Muhammad ascended to heaven), the only person they would obey if he said, "Stop!" is their Mahdi! The treaty is going to say something like, "You stop killing the Muslims and I the Mahdi (Antichrist), and the Muslims will allow you to tear down the Dome of the Rock and build your Temple there and offer your sacrifices in it! How did Daniel know about this treaty over 2,500 years ago?? The Bible's God! How do we know these two witnesses are Enoch and Elijah? That's because they are the only two taken to heaven alive (Gen. 5:24, 2 Kings 2:11). There's no Biblical case where any dead person went to heaven, not even Jesus (Matt. 12:40). So why does 2Corinthians 5:8 say, "We are of good courage, I say, and prefer rather to be absent from the body and to be at home with the Lord." That's because Paradise-Hades is where the righteous go (Luke 23:43), and David (Psalm 139:8) said, "If I make my bed in Sheol (N. T. Hades), behold You are there." So in a special way, Christ presence is in a compartment in the Hades underworld called Paradise. The reason 1 Thess. 4:16-17 says "the dead in Christ," and "we who are alive" will, "meet the Lord in the air and so we shall always be with the Lord," is because the dead are not physically with Him now! When they see what the servants of the King of the Jews do for them, I think many open-minded Muslims will turn to Jesus for their salvation! These Muslims, though some have to die, will know God loves them!

3. Right on time, Many Jews have returned to Israel and have prospered ever since they became a nation in 1948. Without these facts, Bible prophecy could not have been fulfilled.

4. Exactly 1,260 days after he makes the treaty, Antichrist's body will be revived, after being dead, when the spirit of Caesar Nero enters it. This will look like a resurrection; but it's actually a resuscitation! This answers the question, "How does the 666 Antichrist Beast get here?" He will be a "walk-in." The world's leading authority concerning walk-ins, was the late, Ruth Montgomery. In her book, Threshold To Tomorrow, p. 11, she said, we can easily tell they are walk-ins because they have such different personalities than the people who used to live in those bodies. In her 1985 book, Aliens Among Us, p. 12, Montgomery said, "Nowadays it is virtually impossible to pick up any publication in the parapsychology field without running across references to walk-ins, and a number of distinguished psychiatrists and psychologists are exploring the phenomenon as an explanation for their patients' radically altered personalities and goals after a near brush with death." Revelation 17:10-11 says, "And they are seven kings; five have fallen, one is, the other has not yet come; and when he comes, he must remain a little while. The beast which was and is not (and is to come, 17:8), is himself an eighth and is one of the seven, and he goes to destruction." So John writing in about 98 AD, tells us five Antichrists were dead, one is alive, the seventh is yet to come, and his body will also be inhabited by an eighth, which is a king that was alive and now (when John wrote) is dead. Of the seven blasphemous kings (17:3), the five already dead when John wrote, were, Julius Caesar, Tiberius, Caligula, Claudius and Caesar Nero. In both Greek and Hebrew, letters have numerical values. Caesar Nero (616) also called Ceasar Neron (666), is the only possibility here, as his name is the only one that adds up correctly. Our letter for "n" is worth

50. Domitian was the one "alive" when John wrote, and the seventh was to appear at the end. In 13:1, John "saw a beast coming up out of the sea"(Nero was a Gentile, Isaiah 17:12, 57:20)) "that had seven heads", but only the eighth (when he enters the dead body of the seventh), is himself called "the beast." (13:4). And this beast is far more powerful and evil than the original person that occupied his body. In case you doubt he is a different person, Daniel 9:27 says the ruler will make a firm treaty for "seven years," yet we're told the beast only reigns for "forty-two months." (13:1-10). These months are of 30-days and equal 1,260 days; shown by the fact that Enoch and Elijah "will prophesy for 1,260 days, clothed in sackcloth." in the first half of Daniels final seven (Daniel 9:27, Rev. 11:3)). So in the sense that only one body is meant, just one ruler is mentioned. Revelation builds on what Daniel said by providing more details.

5. On the same day Caesar Nero takes over Antichrist's body, he kills Enoch and Elijah. Their dead bodies will lie in a street of Jerusalem for three-and-a-half-days; at which time they will stand on their feet and be raptured to heaven. In their wake a great earthquake will collapse a tenth of the city, killing 7,000 people, leaving everyone terrified and giving "glory to the God of heaven." (11:7-13). By no means does this mean they repented, nor dos it say they did! This is like a forced: "every knee shall bow" (Isaiah 45:23). Romans 14:11 says, "For it is written, 'As I live, says the Lord, every knee shall bow to Me and every tongue shall give praise to God'"

6. On the same day the Antichrist Beast takes over, another beast comes "up out of the earth" (13:11). This beast, being out of the earth, must be a Jew (earthly Temple, kingdom etc), and must be a soul coming out of Hades to enter and revive a dead body, like Nero will. This person, known in the Christian world as "The False Prophet," is most certainly Judas Iscariot.

The Bible only calls two people "son of perdition:" Antichrist in 2 Thess. 2:3 and Judas in John 17:12. This False Prophet will perform all sorts of miracles including making, "fire come down out of heaven to the earth in the presence of men," and giving "breath to the image of the (Antichrist) beast, so that the image of the beast would even speak and cause as many as do not worship the image of the beast to be killed. And he causes all, the small and the great, the rich and the poor, and the free men and the slaves, to be given a mark on their right hand or on their forehead And no one will be able to buy or sell except the one who has the mark; the name of the beast or the number of his name." (13:13-17).

7. The most difficult thing for me to believe, until recently, was that "They worshiped the Dragon!" (13:4). Much of society is now so uneducated, deceived, and desperate, that I can see it happening!

8. The coming of the Jewish King, and therefore, New Year's Day in the year zero, according to Harold W. Hoehner (Chronological Aspects Of The Life Of Christ), happened on March 30, AD 33. All of this is based on there being 2,000 years between the Jews needing to be spiritually revived and them being revived! Hosea 6:1-2 says, "Yahweh … will revive us in two days" Then Peter said, "with the Master (Greek Kurios), one day is like a thousand years." The reason I know this 2,000 years is spiritual, is because the Jews were physically scattered in AD 70 and regathered into a nation in 1948 which is far less than 2,000. In addition they were not "revived" in 1948! The need to be spiritually revived came at the Triumphal Entry when "He approached (Jerusalem), He saw the city and wept over it, saying, 'If you had known this your day, even you, the things which make for peace! But now they have been hidden from your eyes." (Luke 19:41-42). Yes! This was their day-- New Years Day in the year zero! The revival of the only Jews

left on Earth, will come when Jesus returns: "I will pour out on the house of David and on the inhabitants of Jerusalem, the Spirit of grace and of supplication, so that they will look upon Me Whom they have pierced; and they will morn for Him as one mourns for an only son, and they will weep bitterly over Him like the bitter weeping over a firstborn." (Zechariah 12:10). "Yahweh ... will remove from your midst, your proud, exalting ones, and you will never again be haughty on My holy mountain. (Zephaniah 3:8,11). With all the proud Jews gone, "all Israel will be saved' for He "will remove ungodliness from Jacob." (Romans 11:26). The number of Jews to be saved at this end-time revival is 144,000--12,000 from each tribe (Revelation 7:4-8). Daniel 9:25 says, "So you are to know and discern that from the issuing of a decree to restore and rebuild Jerusalem until Messiah the Prince,there will be seven weeks and sixty-two weeks." According to Hoehner and The Bible Knowledge Commentary (Dallas), Nehemiah's decree happened on March 5, 444 BC and therefore 476 years and 25 days later (one year between BC 1 and AD 1), brings us to March 30, 33 AD for Christ's Triumphal Entry into Jerusalem. This requires translating the 483-360-day prophetic-years into 365 day years with the needed leap year days included. Zachariah agrees, the coming of the Jewish King was not His birth, but his Triumphal Entry! "Rejoice greatly, O daughter of Zion! Shout O daughter of Jerusalem! Behold your King is coming to you! He is just and endowed with salvation! Humble, and mounted on a donkey, even the colt, the foal of a donkey." (Zec. 9:9). Hosea 6:2 says, "He will revive us after two days." 2 Peter 3:8 says, "with the Lord one day is as 1,000 years." So moving forward, we must subtract 75 days from March 30, 2033 to find the most likely day for Christ's return! That's because it takes Jesus 75 days to judge the world, revive the 144,000 Jews and establish His Kingdom. That's why Revelation has

1,260 days between the 666 Antichrist's takeover and Christ's return (Rev. 12:6, 13:5, 19:11-20), whereas Daniel 12:12 says, "How blessed is he who keeps waiting and attains to the 1,335 days."(Dan. 12:12). So by subtracting 75 days from March 30, 2033, we arrive at January 14, 2033 for Christ's return in this scenario! Regardless, everyone paying attention will know Jesus returns 5,250 days after Enoch and Elijah arrive! Working back 5,250 days from January 14, 2033, we arrive at February 19, 2026 (1993 in real time). One thing is certain: the Temple will be built where the Dome of the Rock is before our eyes, very soon!

KNOWING THE BIBLE'S GOD IN THE LITTLE TIME WE HAVE

(CAN'T BE LAZY)

The one rational thing we must do in this insane world, is to **get to know God.** In the little time we have, we must **find God.** Or at least we must **ask God to find us.** But how can we ever know Him? One thing's for sure: it doesn't just happen! There are prerequisites! God chooses whom He wants! Here is my advice!

1) **Work Hard and Fast.** I'm sure most of you find this to be a surprising first step. One of the seven deadly sins is "slothfulness." "Idleness is the devil's workshop." "Even your own prophets say, "Cretans are always liars, evil-beasts, lazy-gluttons." (Titus 1:12). It's normal for those who "have too much time on their hands" to sink into all kinds of sins. They come to expect everything to be handed to them and when they don't get their way they tend to blame God. They think God (and others), should serve them! They think they are owed. When they are cast into the eternal lake of fire, they will blame God forever! They will not understand why they are punished! "None of the wicked will understand." (Daniel 12:10).

If I were running a country, I would make it mandatory that all able-bodied people have a job to do. Everybody should do something. Children should have chores. I think anybody living off handouts, will be ruined before long. Even retired people, to retain their mental and physical health, should stay busy. The handicapped should do what they can, even if it's just mental work.

Jesus said, "The Son of Man (His favorite way of referring to Himself), did not come to be served, but to serve." (Matt. 20:28). And again, "Unto this very hour My Father is working and I Am working." (John 5:17). Before Adam sinned, God gave him a job to do. He was to cultivate the Garden of Eden and guard it. (Genesis 2:15).

Peter was called while working as a fisherman, and became a fisher of men. John the Beloved Apostle was called while mending fishing nets, and he tied up lose-ends in the fourth Gospel. Gideon was called while thrashing wheat and became a "valiant warrior" who delivered Israel by thrashing the Midianites and Amalekites. (Judges 6:11-8:28). Billy Graham (fastest milker in NC), was called while milking cows and he milked every venue to preach the Gospel to the world!

For the Christian, working hard is a form of discipline and suffering. Many of you hate your job. But you shouldn't, because God is training you. The Bible says we should "be thankful for all things." We are working for God, no matter who our earthly boss may be (Colossians 3:23).

Even Jesus was required to be a carpenter (probably a stone mason actually). Working was part of the suffering (and I say this knowing I'm treading on hollowed ground), He needed to become the Man He became. The Apostle Paul put it this way, "Though He were a Son, yet learned He obedience through the things which He suffered." (Hebrews 5:8). Revelation 14:13 says, "And I heard a voice from heaven, saying, 'Write, Blessed are the dead who die in the Lord from now on!' 'Yes,' says the Spirit, 'so they may rest from their labors, for their deeds follow with them.'"

There's something about working hard that makes it possible for you to receive God's light. D. L. Moody, a forerunner of Billy Graham, said, "I've never heard of a lazy person who received Jesus Christ as their Lord."

2) **Humble Yourself.** You cannot come to God waving your PH. D. or any other source of pride! "And He (Jesus) called a child to Himself and set him before them, and said, 'Truly I say to you, unless you are converted and become like children, you will not enter the kingdom of heaven. Whoever then humbles himself as this child, he is greatest in the kingdom of heaven." (Matthew 18:2-4). Pride is the greatest sin, and it keeps more people from knowing God than any other sin.

3) **Pray For Yourself.** I cannot guarantee you will be saved from the **ETERNAL LAKE OF FIRE** because of prayer, but I can guarantee you'll be there a trillion years from now, if nobody prays for you. Nobody knows just exactly how prayer works? But we do know nothing eternally-good ever comes about without it. You cannot always depend on others to pray for you, so you should pray for yourself. You may say, "I don't believe in God." Then pray' "Oh God, if You're there, hear my prayer, reveal Yourself to me, and save me from my sins and help me turn away from them." Pray, "Draw me after you, and let us run together!" (The Song of Solomon 1:4).

Prayer is needed because no matter how brilliant you are, you cannot find God by searching with your mind. He must *reveal* Himself to you in some way, deep in your heart. God is far beyond comprehension for the natural, unaided mind. Even Einstein was unable to understand Him or find Him, though he saw evidence of His vast mind. "The natural man, is not able to comprehend the things of God because, they are spiritually discerned." (I Corinthians 2:14).

Let me leave you with words we should all read or recite every day: "And if anyone's name was not found written in the Book-of-Life, he was thrown into the lake of fire!" (Rev. 20:15). "Behold I Am coming quickly, and My reward is with Me, to give to every man according to what he has done" (Rev. 22:12). "Let the one who wishes, take the water of life without cost." (Rev. 22:17).

SPELLING AND WRITING/A BONUS FOR YOU

I wrote 34 articles for the Poughkeepsie Journal about honey bees, bumble bees and yellowjackets. I was helped by top experts: Thomas D. Seeley (honey bees), Robbin W. Thorp (bumble bees), and John W. Wenzel and James M. Carpenter (yellowjackets). These are the entomologists other entomologists turn to for information. I was shocked by the fact that they spelled these three insects different than the dictionaries?? Finally I asked Robbin about it! His answer was even more shocking: "That's because the dictionaries don't know how to spell insects' names." Then he proceeded to prove it, by saying: "If it's a bee, it must be two words--bumble bee! I've been fighting with magazine editors all my life!" Immediately I realized he was arguing with the wrong people, and I proceeded to contact Britannica's reader's editor, John Cunningham called me (Jan. 16, 2015), after looking into this, and said, "Almost every entomologist I could find and the Entomological Society of America confirmed what you said and our online version now includes their way of spelling these three words." The rule for spelling insects is very simple: "If it's a bee it must be two words--honey bee. If it's a fly it must be two words--house fly, sweat fly etc.! If it's not a fly, then one word--butterfly, dragonfly etc.! So to spell it "yellow jacket," like the dictionaries, is to say it's a jacket that's yellow, so it must be "yellowjacket." Most major dictionaries now include the correct spellings! For a deeper look into this see my: "Bumblebee or Bumble Bee/Poughkeepsie Journal."

Now let me help with some mistakes I often hear or read. It is incorrect to say: "an historical." It must be "a historical." It is wrong to say, "hit the ball further" or "further down the road," because "further" isn't about distance. For distance, you must use, "farther." "Further" is used for abstract things, like "further thought" or "further studies." You cannot say, "this or that might happen," or "I might go to the store." That's because, "might" is past tense! You must say "I may do this or that." When you write, you must say everything in as few words as possible, so the reader doesn't get bored by words that don't help! You should not say, "the sun is shinning brightly." To say, "The sun is bright," carries the same meaning. When you think most of your readers understand what you've said, don't bore them by explaining yourself to the others.

SEVENTEEN

Who Wrote Revelation?
They're Saying The Apostle John Didn't Write Like This

I WAS TAUGHT, REVELATION WAS WRITTEN BY JOHN, THE BELOVED Apostle. I was taught he had his favorite words (Greek) and subjects and it was obvious the person who wrote the Gospel of John also wrote Revelation. Watchman Nee, the greatest Bible teacher I ever read, claims there's no doubt. The fact that he simply calls himself "john" tells me it cannot be anybody else. Any other John would've given us additional information about himself. Of course, John the Baptist was dead. So I've been baffled by documentaries claiming John the Beloved Apostle couldn't have written Revelation, because it was written in a style too different from his other writings. I didn't believe them, but wondered what could be causing their conclusion.

In approximately AD 262, about 1666 years after Revelation, Dionysius, Bishop of Alexandria, commented on Revelation's authorship (Ante-Nicene Fathers, Vol. 6 pg. 84). To my utter amazement, he did not believe the John who wrote Revelation was the Beloved Apostle!? He points out that there are no language errors in te Gospel or Epistle of John, which were written. "with the greatest elegance, both in their expressions and in their reasonings, and in the whole structure of their style. For, as might be presumed, the writer possessed the gift of both kinds of discourse, the Lord having bestowed both these capacities upon him--that of knowledge and of expression." Dionysius contrasts this author, with the writer of Revelation: "his dialect language are not of the exact Greek type, and he employs barbarous idioms, and in some places also solecisms" (mistakes in grammar, language and word usage).

So now I see why scholars don't think John the Beloved Apostle wrote Revelation. But I don't understand why the very best scholars, including Watchman NEE and nearly all the church-leaders that followed the Apostles, thought he did?

Right on time for this treatise, I stumbled upon the answer while looking through my great-grandparents The Family Bible (of all places!). "The book was written by St. John, the Apostle, as is proved by ample and satisfactory evidence." "Zucke has also collected internal evidence to show that the original is the Greek of a Jewish Christian. Zucke has also examined in minute detail the peculiarities of language which obviously distinguish the Revelation from every other book of the New Testament. And in subsequent sections he urges with great force the difference between the Revelation on the one side and the fourth Gospel and the first Epistle on the other in respect of their style and composition and the mental character and attainments of the writer of each. Hengstenberg, in a dissertation, appended to his commentary, maintains that they are by one writer. It may be admitted that the Revelation has many surprising grammatical peculiarities. But much of this is accounted for by the fact it was probably written down as it was seen 'in the spirit,' whilst the ideas, in all their novelty and vastness, filled the Apostle's mind and rendered him less capable of attending to forms of speech. His great desire was to deliver his wonderful message, and the phraseology of his writing became a matter of secondary importance,"

John was filled with amazement and awe! And no doubt, he was somewhat rattled! Do you think you'd write exactly as usual, if you were just taken to heaven and shown the Revelation like John was???

When Daniel was through seeing a vision of Antichrist, he said, "My thoughts were greatly alarming me and my face turned pale"

(Dan. 7:28). After seeing an additional vision of this powerful world-ruler and his kingdom, Daniel said, "Then I Daniel fainted and was sick for days" and "I was astounded by the vision" (Dan. 8:27) So theses visions can take it out of a person!

Another reason John didn't write exactly in his usual way is because, he was out of his body most of the time when he saw the future. I've heard several people in the paranormal field incorrectly use Revelation 1:10 to prove John was out of his body when he received the Revelation. That verse says, "I was in the Spirit on the Lord's day." This simply means John was close to God and fellowshipping with Him on Sunday. See Galatians 5:16, Acts 20:7 and 1 Cor. 16:2.. Under "LORD'S DAY," in A DICTIONARY of EARLY CHRISTIAN BELIEFS (David W. Bercot, Editor), it says, "What today is commonly referred to as Sunday was usually called the Lord's Day by early Christians." The first day of the week was when Christians gathered to hear whoever had a message from God, and to break bread and give as we "may prosper" (Acts 20:7, ! Cor. 16:1-2). We are to devote the first day of the week to The Lord, so if we get busy in other ways the other six days, at least one day will be totally The Lord's. That's not to say we shouldn't be worshiping Him, thanking Him, trusting Him and witnessing every day (1 Thessalonians 5:18, Hebrews 11:6, Luke 4:8, Genesis 22:5, Acts 20:19-21).

In chapter four we find something different has happened. John sees a door open in heaven, and says, "Suddenly I became in the spirit." Then he starts to describe the scene in heaven including seeing God on His throne. It's obvious he left his body and went flying through the open door he saw in heaven. Becoming "in spirit" in chapter four cannot refer to walking close to God, because John was already "in the spirit" in that sense in 1:10. At this point in his life, John was probably always close to the Lord.

Revelation teaches us that life in our soul dimension is physical in that realm. Though John was in his spirit-body, yet he could see, hear, talk, have memory, weep, and yes, even write and be seen and recognized by the beings in heaven (Rev. 4:2-8, 5:4-5, 6:10-11) This is confirmed by Jesus in the story of the rich man and Laazarus (Luke 16:19-31) Though dead, the rich man had "eyes," and a "tongue," could see, had memory, could speak and suffered in a flame of fire that did not consume him. In this realm we are indestructible, can feel heat, and can suffer forever. Jesus warned of a place, "where the worm doesn't die and the fire is not quenched" (Mark 9:44,48). The Apostle Paul must've often left his body: "I know a man in Christ who 14 years ago--whether in the body I do not know, or out of the body I do not know; God knows--such a man was caught up to the third heaven." (2 Cor. 12:2). There are thousands of modern cases of people floating out of their bodies during operations. Though sometimes blood wasn't flowing to the brain, yet they could see, hear and remember. The most famous was that of a patient whose soul went up on the hospital roof and saw a red shoe. Someone went and sure enough it was there! If you ask your friends, it won't be long before someone will have a story about how they left the body!

Some mystics say they can see a soul outside the body, connected to the body by a silver cord. They say when the cord snaps the person dies. This agrees with Ecclesiastes 12:6-7, "The silver cord is broken ... then the dust will return to the earth."

John did not receive the Revelation and later write what he heard and saw. No! He wrote as he went along. John, still out of his physical body in 10:4, said, "I was about to write." In 14:13 "a voice out of heaven" told him to "write." In19:5,9 "a voice" that "came out of the throne" said, "write," and 21:5 says, "He that sat on the throne said, "write." I think there's a good chance John used a golden pen, similar to the one the giant man (angel) in paradise used to write the record of our lives (see The Testament of Abraham, recension B, chapter 10, translated ny Michael E. Stone).

So the content he related and the fact that John was out of his body while he wrote, effected his writing of Revelation. John wrote as he went along, not having time to compose himself. I think the reason he didn't go back and polish what he wrote was because, he wanted us to feel the full-force of the awesome-effect of what he saw and heard. He wanted us to experience some of the effect it had on him.

In light of how this partial end-time-picture affected Daniel, it's quite certain the full-Revelation the aged-Apostle saw, would've cost him his life had he been in his body. That probably explains why God brought him to heaven "in the spirit" to show him the Revelation.

DOCUMENTARIES ARE SAYING THE APOSTLE WOULD'VE BEEN TOO OLD TO HAVE WRITTEN REVELATION

I will admit he would've been at least nearly 90 and maybe 100. And yes, I can understand why scholars find it hard to believe a man of his age culd've survived being exiled to the desolate--Island of Patmos, where he fled for his life for preaching the Gospel (Rev. 1:9). Watchman Nee and G H. Pember both quoted Tertullian, "the Apostle John, after having been plunged into boiling oil without suffering any harm, was banished to an island." Patmos is just a huge rock, with no plants; but though the old-man suffered, God was with him. In his book "Chief Men Among the Brethren," Hy Pickering tells of several preachers who were still serving God in their 90s. He said this of P. G. Anderson, who died in 1907 at 97, "Thus throughout a life prolonged to an unusual period, our friend was ever assiduous to do the Lord's work, whether as an evangelist, as a pastor, or as a pattern to the flock." The world-famous-preacher, George Muller, served God until he died at 93 in 1898 Pickering wrote, "The previous day had seen him busy at his ordinary occupation, and in the evening he had taken his usual part in the prayer meeting."

God strengthens those who love Him, serve Him and seek Him. "those who trust in the Lord will be newly-strengthened. They will mount up with wings like eagles. They will run and not be tired, they will walk and not get weary." (Deut. 34:7). It also may be God used angels to help John.

NOW THEY'RE SAYING JOHN COULDN'T WRITE

I've long felt it's important to answer objections to my beliefs. A 2008 documentary said, John the Beloved Apostle couldn't have written Revelation because, he couldn't write They quoted Acts 4:13 as proof- -"But seeing the boldness of Peter and John, and perceiving that they were unlettered and uneducated men, they wondered; and they recognized them, that they had been with Jesus."

Apparently these, Apostle-John-wrote-Revelation debunkers, don't talk to one another!!? How can one argument be that the author of Revelation didn't write like the Apostle John and another argument be that he couldn't write???

Peter and John may have been fishermen, but it's obvious they were well-versed in the Scriptures (the Old Testament) It was God who brought the needed Scriptures to their memories as they spoke The Apostle Paul said, "Not that we are competent of ourselves to think anything as of ourselves, but our competency is of God, who has also made us able ministers of the New Covenant" (2 Cor, 3:5-6).

But if they were never memorized, these verses wouldn't be available for God to direct them to use. Peter, who was lumped together with John as "unlettered and uneducated," showed his vast knowledge by proclaiming how "all the prophets" told of Christ's suffering and that Moses said, all must listen to Him (Acts chapter three).

The world-renowned Bible-scholar, F. F. Bruce (in his Bible commentary, p. 1276), sheds light on this subject. "The rulers' estimate of Peter and John as 'uneducated laymen' reflects the spiritual pride of the professionals in Theology, but does not mean what many readers of the A. V. suppose. The skill and power of Peter's defense were admitted, but as the Apostles had not been trained in rabbinical schools, their obvious capacity was due to their training in the unofficial school of Jesus."

It's no wonder the Apostles taught with boldness, unlike the professionals, for Jesus, their Teacher, "taught them as having authority and not as their scribes" (Mark 1:22).

It is absolutely certain John knew how to write. In his first Epistle he said, "I write to you" or "I have written to you" 11 times.

Why do some feel it's so important to try to prove John the Beloved Apostle didn't write Revelation? I guess they think it will lessen the impact? If some other John wrote it, Revelation would give him credibility, but if John wrote it, that would give Revelation additional authority.

THE APOSTLE JOHN RESTED ON
JESUS' BOSOM (JOHN 13:33)

(THE ONE PLACE IN THE UNIVERSE
WE CAN FIND TRUE REST)

In the past 40 years, every time I've gotten to 1:17-18, while reciting Revelation, I've always wondered why Jesus didn't say, "I'm the One Whose bosom you rested on?" John had just seen Jesus in His judgment mode, "His eyes were like a flame of fire; and His feet were like burnished bronze, when it has been made to glow in a furnace, and His voice was like the roar of many waters. And in His right hand He held seven stars; and out of His mouth came a sharp two-edged sword; and His face was like the sun shinning in its strength And when I saw Him, I fell at His feet as a dead man" (1:14-17a).

At this point, in order to relieve John's fear, we find, "And He laid His right hand upon me, saying, 'Do not be afraid; I Am the first and the last and the living One; and I was dead, and look I am alive forevermore; and I have the keys of death and Hades'" (1:17b-18).

Now you can see why, when I get to this place while reciting Revelation, the question always flashes, "Why didn't Jesus say, ''I'm the One Whose bosom you rested on?'"

I was rather stunned to find that Irenaeus, who as a boy heard Polycarp, a disciple of John's, teach; relate the following. "When John could not endure the sight (for he says, 'I fell at His feet as dead') the Word (Jesus) reviving him, and reminding him that it was He upon whose bosom he had leaned at supper" (Ante-Nicene Fathers Vol. 1, page 491).

I do not know how or why this escaped being included in Revelation? But the fact that Polycarp, apparently heard it directly from the Apostle, and was heard to have said so by Iranaeus, is powerful evidence that Revelation was indeed written by the Beloved Apostle John.

According to The Companion Bible, Melito, Bishop of Sardis (c.170); Eusebius and Irenaeus (c180); the Moratorium canon fragment and Clement (c200); Tertullian (c.220); Origen (c.233); and Hippolytus all thought John the Beloved Apostle wrote Revelation This pushes the conclusion beyond a reasonable doubt!

It's Been Said, "Truth Is Stranger Than Fiction." When It Comes To Weird, Mysterious Or Paranormal Subjects; Skeptics' Explanations Are:

EIGHTEEN

Stranger Than Truth
(Skeptics In Only One Direction)
(They Only See What They Want To See)

IN THIS DAY AND AGE, WITH INFORMATION EASILY ACCESSIBLE, skeptics don't believe in mysterious events or things, such as;animal mutilations; shapeshifters; haunted houses; spontaneous-human-combustion; ghosts; automatic-writing; mothman;levitation; men-in-black;angels; telepathy; psychokinesis; near-death-experiences; out-of-body-experiences;demon possession; UFO-abductions by humanoid beings, different looking (grays etc.), smarter and with abilities far beyond our own; extremely-high-tech crop-circles; bigfoot-creatures; ancient high-technology; creation by The Bible's all-knowing, all-powerful and unimaginably-skillful God; unlearned-knowledge; or Bible prophecy???? How is it that these intelligent people can be so unaware of what's going on? The truth terrifies them into making up scenarios that are often stranger than the the facts they are trying to debunk! Delve deeply into any of these subjects and you will find a mystery! Skeptics never see one because: 1) They never agree with the experts! There are people who've spent 30-50 years researching things like UFO abductions, crop circles etc.; and skeptics think if they study for a couple of years or less, often without interviewing anyone, they can sit back in their easy-chairs and say, "Nope! It can't be!" 2) Skeptics never apply Occam's Razor! For example, when it comes to multiple-personalities, the plain, simple answer is that there are more than one person (or demons), inside that body! Often even the voice is different! But they believe wild, complicated psychological problems produce other personalities, not believing what Jesus taught about demon possession. (Luke 8:30). 3) They do little or no field research! 4) They are in this ignorant-condition, is due to the fact that, instead of searching for truth, their goal is to debunk! If they actually went into real crop circles, they'd know the technology involved if far beyond anything that can be done with boards and ropes! People with boards and ropes can duplicate a design, but cannot weave the plants or bend them a foot off the ground by microwaving and melting . There are formations made by balls of light, while people were watching! Formations have been made in muddy fields, with no signs of tracts or any sort of disturbance! Phones don't work in these circles! Man-made circles aren't PERFECTLY-round, like the real ones! (see Mysterious Lights and Crop Circles, by Linda Moulton Howe).

Skeptics do not believe any of what hundreds of millions of people say they saw! Nor do they believe what radar and sonar have seen!

A large black cat transformed into a bipedal human-like animal with a "terrible grin" (SHAPESHIFTERS Morphing Monsters & Changing Cryptids by Nick Redfern p. 70).

Bigfoot-creatures can talk to us telepathically, speak English and shoot a flashlight-like beam out of their eyes, disappear into dimensions outside of our perception and are associated with UFOs (The Quantum Bigfoot by Ron Morehead).

Creationists are skeptical of the theory of evolution! Common people are skeptical of evolution! Evolutionists are skeptical of evolution! The ONLY people who are not skeptical of evolution are the skeptics!! I've read hundreds of skeptic magazines, and I have never seen an article skeptic of the theory of evolution??? They have "believing brains!" They've been taught, "what to think," and not, "how to think!" They are not skeptics! They are atheists or agnostics and evolutionists!

Men-in-black can vanish, make their eyes glow like flaslights and are connected to UFOs and mothman (The Real Men in Black by Nick Redfern).

In the February 1, 2011 issue of Scientific American, world-famous-skeptic, Michael Shermer, wrote an article titled: "Houdini's Skeptical Advice: Just Because Something's Unexplained Doesn't Mean It's Supernatural." I happened to have read a book that had the incident Shermer talked about. What Shermer failed to say, was that Arthur Conan Doyle believed that Houdini did some of his tricks by using help from the spirit world. With the background in place, "Houdini had Conan Doyle hang a slate from anywhere in the room so that it was free to swing in space." Doyle was told to go somewhere and write something on "a piece of paper" and "put it back in his pocket and return to the house." Houdini had Doyle "scoop up the (white) ink-soaked (cork) ball in a spoon and place it against the slate, where it wrote "the entire phrase," and "dropped to the ground." Shermer left out the fact that Doyle said, "I got you now Houdini--that was no trick!" But Shermer's conclusion, of course, was that it was just a trick as Houdini insisted.

So I went to Shermer's web site and gave him my "Gullible Person of the Year" award for believing Houdini! I said, "Houdini wouldn't trick you, now would he?"

This was a form of automatic-writing, which is always associated with the spirit-world! It looks like the demons played a little trick on Houdini! Of all things Doyle, and therefore the ball could've written; it was exactly the same thing king Belshazzar saw when, "Suddenly the fingers of a man's hand emerged and began writing opposite the lampstand on the plaster of the wall of the king's palace, and the king saw the back of the hand that did the writing. Then the king's face grew pale and his thoughts alarmed him, and his joints went slack and his knees began knocking together." (Daniel 5:5-6). What the hand, Doyle and the ball all wrote was, "MENE MENE TEKEL UPHARSIN," and Daniel told king Belshazzar, it meant, "your kingdom is history!"

(5:25) "That same night Belshazzar the Chaldean king was slain." (5:30). Daniel had told him, "you have exalted yourself against THE HIGH EXALTED ONE (lord), (Mareh). Isaiah 33:5 says, "Yahweh is exalted, for He dwells on high." This story is where we got the expression: "The handwriting is on the wall!"

Here is my challenge to all skeptics! Search-the-world-over and bring me a person who can do that automatic-writing trick, and show us how it was done! I already KNOW it is impossible! If it were were a trick, to shut-Doyle-up, Houdini would've shown him how he did it! When Houdini was lowered into a body of water, handcuffed and in a box-chained-shut, he escaped with the handcuffs and the box still closed. This was done when his body dematerialized and went through the cuffs and the box, reassembling on the outside. This is logically the only way it could be done and so far no other magician has duplicated this "trick." To call these two wonders, "tricks," is to make the explanation harder to believe than the events themselves! The explanations are "stranger-than-science!"

ONLY THE BIBLE HAS MADE ACCURATE PREDICTIONS 2,500 YEARS AHEAD OF TIME

When Daniel saw over 2,500 years into the future, he didn't understand the astonishing technology he saw! He said, "Many will zoom back and forth and knowledge will multiply" (Dan. 12:4).

EUPHORIA TO APORIA

(The USA in the Last Days)

(The Last Days of the USA)

In Luke 21:25, Jesus said, in the last days there would be "distress among nations in perplexity" (Greek--"aporia"). Lamentations 4:5

will be enacted in the USA, starting in the 2020s--"Those who ate delicacies are desolate in the streets! Those reared in purple embrace ash pits!" "Aporia" means, "nobody has an answer," thus "perplexity." We are almost there! As I write, it's March of 2023, (almost New Years Day in the real 1990). So we have 10 years left, the final three and a half will be the worst in the history of the universe! Jesus said, ""For then there will be great tribulation such as has not occured since the beginning of the world until now, nor ever will. (Matt24:21). Concerning the last days, in 1966 it was thought: 1) The Antichrist would arise in the UN, 2) There would be a one-world government, and 3) The USA would be in ruins. In 2010 I wrote, "On page 94 of my 1990 book, Insanity Strikes the Diamond, I said, "The times ahead will be far worse than any of us can imagine. By 2033 the human race will be on the verge of total annihilation. (Christ will return to prevent it--Matt 24:22). The focus at the end will be on Jerusalem."

The USA leads the way in killing unborn babies! In January of 2019 the passing of New York's, Reproductive Health Act, brought about a standing ovation in the Senate chamber, because it legalized abortion until birth for any reason. The One World Trade Center was lit in pink! New York State is already in deep trouble! And we haven't seen anything yet! Many of our cities will soon be rubble from earthquakes and washed away in tsunamis! John said, "I heard a voice in the center of the four living creatures saying, 'A quart of wheat for a day's pay, and three quarts of barley for a day's pay; and do not spill the oil or the wine." (Revelation 6:6). Mark my words, "Starvation diets will be here in less than 10 years; Christianity will be outlawed in the USA, similar to in China; the Antichrist will arise out of the USA; and there will be, at the most, only one more presidential election."

Pergamum was "Where Satan's throne" was (Rev. 2:13). Now he resides in the USA; ground zero for abortions, pornography, laziness, gluttony, drug abuse, and haters of God. We are in the violence of the days of Noah (Luke 17:26, Gen. 6:13). Jesus is in control and the "time to tear apart" (Ecclesiastes 3:7), has arrived! The cosmos is passing away! Cast yourself into Christ's arms before it's too late!

"Then what shall we do?" When the crowds asked John The Baptist, He said, "Let the one who has two shirts give to him who has none; and he who has food is to do likewise." (Luke 3:10-11). In order to live like that, we must obey the two great commandments: "You shall love the Lord your God with all your heart, with all your soul and with all your mind," and "You shall love your neighbor as yourself." (Deuteronomy 6:5, Leviticus 19:18, Matt. 22:35-40).

NINETEEN

The Triumph Of Jacob, Who Wrestled With His Creator

I'VE FOUND IN GENESIS, 20 DEALINGS, OR SHOULD I SAY, TRIALS, Jacob endured before he "triumphed." He was a cheater and schemer, who always tried to get the most out of every situation. So God had to arrange things so that Jacob's plans often backfired. In this way, God was weakening him enough so that He could finally win His life-long wrestling match with this difficult character, we know as Jacob. He and his brother "struggled together" in Rebekah's womb (25:22). Their father, Isaac, "loved Esau" making Jacob the dark sheep of the family (25:28). Jacob served Laban 14 years so he could marry his daughter, Rachel (29:20-30). "Rachel was barren" for several years (29:31). Rachel upset Jacob, by saying, "Give me children or I will die." (30:1). "You know I served your father with all my strength, yet you father cheated me and changed my wages ten times (so 10 trials, 31:6,7). Rachel caused Jacob and Laban to quarrel by stealing her father's idols (36:31). "By day the the heat consumed me, and the frost by night; and my sleep fled from my eyes" (31:40). Jacob "was greatly afraid and distressed," for his life to know his long-lost brother Esau, whom he cheated greatly, was "coming to meet" him with "400 men" (32:6-7). In this time of deep distress, he met God that night and "wrestled with Him until dawn" (32:24). "He touched the socket of his thigh; so the socket of Jacob's thigh was dislocated" (32:25), and "he was limping on his thigh" the rest of his life (32:31).

I want to look further into this vitally important event of Jacob's wrestling with God in Genesis32.

They wrestled all night until daybreak and these two loved one another, "Jacob have I loved" (Romans 9:13).

In every sense, God won this wrestling match. It was Jacob who left, "limping on his thigh" (32:32). Yet amazingly, The Bible says, God said, "you have striven with God and prevailed." (32:28).

What can be the meaning of such a statement? It's gonna take a genius, with spiritual discernment to figure this one out. Destiny has provided one,from China--no less! He was an unusual genius. His official name was Nee To-sheng. But the Chinese often look at what happens on the day a baby is born to find a nickname. On the night Nee was born, God arranged it for a watchman to continuously pass by his mother's hospital room. Thus, the man who would become one of the greatest watchers of people's souls, got his nickname! His death in 1972, was announced on Billy Graham's weekly radio program, "The Hour of Decision." To this very day, almost everywhere The Bible is taught, quotes from his dozens of books are attributed to, the world-renowned--Watchman Nee!

He spent the final 20 years of his life in prison for preaching the Gospel in China. I was in a little church service where his colleague, Stephen Kaung, read a letter from Nee in prison. Kaung wept when he got to where Nee said, "I know how to maintain my joy." In "From Glory To Glory, p. 157, Nee said, "Once I had people pointing a gun at me, forbidding me to preach Jesus. But I would rather be shot than not to speak about Christ." Oh how true that, "the world is not worthy" of such men (Hebrews 11:38).

Now back to why it can be said, "Jacob triumphed?" The gist of what Watchman Nee said, is: "When God completely, and totally, and utterly, finally defeats you and grinds you to dust and touches you in such a way that you can never again be the old self-serving, self-reliant, full of your own-scheming and planning self. When He at long-last is able to blast you to pieces, so you can never again be hard on people, nervous, and untrusting. When He fundamentally touches you (the thigh is the strongest part of the flesh), so that from now on you "limp" up to people, exuding peace, love and joy; so that now you are able to bless people and not care whether you are happy or even whether you live or die. Yes, when God completely defeated Jacob--and only then, could it be said, Jacob "prevailed!"

When God gets100% of us, then we have, "prevailed."

Before this wrestling match, Jacob didn't trust God like he should. His brother, whom he wronged greatly years earlier, was coming to meet him with 400 men (32:6). Jacob made elaborate plans and was going to be way back in line when Esau arrived. Jacob "was greatly afraid and distressed" (32:7). All his plans are in 32:8-20.

But after he wrestled with God, he went, "limping on his thigh" (32:32). All was very different now. He trusted God and had a "holy indifference" to events. Now he walked ahead of everyone to meet Esau in peace (33:3). Now he could say, "Yea though I walk through the valley of the shadow of death, I will fear no harm, for You are with me." (Psalm 23:4). Now he said to Esau, "I see your face as one sees the face of God" (33:10). When we are sensitive and of "a broken and contrite heart" (Psalm 51:17), we see the faces of those we've wronged, as if we're seeing the face of God, because we are convicted of our sin against those people. It's as if we're looking into the face of God and His look is asking us: "What about this?" We know we must apologize and pay them back as we can, which Jacob did (33:11). Did we apologize to anyone today? Maybe we are in darkness? I only know of two people who apologized to everyone they knew--Watchman Nee and Billy Graham!

As they wrestled all night, I'd love to know the conversation. I think God was teling him the reason for all the trials he endured and how much He, in His great love, arranged them. The Jewish community, though not mentioned in Genesis, knew tat Jacob wept bittersweet tears of repentance and joy all night. Many years later, this was committed to Scripture by Hosea in 12:4-5, "Yes he wrestled with the Messenger and prevailed; he wept and sought His favor. He found him at Bethel and there He spoke with us. Even Yahweh, the Eloheem of hosts! Yahweh is His name."

The reason Jacob said, "I will not let You go unless you bless me," is because now, he no longer looked to the world for joy and satisfaction; but said in his heart, "Whom have I in heaven and besides You, I desire nothing on Earth." (Psalm 73:25).

Sometimes we think we could've planned our lives better than God has. All the many trials Jacob endured, gave him the capacity to understand and yield to God.

Bob Mumford was asked, "Why did the Israelites have to roam the desert for 40 years?" Bob said, "Because God couldn't accomplish what He wanted to work into their lives in 39." When the 40 years were finally over, God spoke of, "the day I brought them out of the land of Egypt, from the iron furnace." (Jeremiah 11:4). "But Yahweh has taken you out of the iron furnace, from Egypt, to be a people for His own possession, as today." (Deuteronomy 4:20).

Peter said, "In this you greatly rejoice, even though now for a little while, if necessary, you have been distressed by various trials, so that the proof of your faith, being more precious than gold which is perishable, even though tested by fire, may be found to result in praise and glory and honor at the revelation of Jesus Christ." (1 Peter 1:6-7).

Though Jacob had triumphed, he continued to experience trials as part of his life. That's because God continues His life-long work on all of us. But a certain gentleness, unknown before, can now be seen in how Jacob expressed his various disappointments. Hebrews 12:11 says, "All discipline for the moment seems not to be joyful, but sorrowful; yet to those who have been trained by it, afterwards it yields the peaceful fruit of righteousness." And after all, how can we complain, when it was said of Christ, "Although He was a Son, He learned obedience from the things which He suffered." (Heb. 5:8).

Now let's look at the trials Jacob endured after he wrestled with God and "prevailed." His daughter, Dinah, was "raped by force" (34:2). His sons caused him "trouble" when they "looted the city" because of Dinah (34:27, 30). His beloved wife, Rachel, died giving birth to Benjamin (35:19), causing Jacob deep "sorrow" (48:7). Jacob is led to believe his beloved son, "Joseph has surely been torn to pieces" by a "wild beast" and he "refused to be comforted" saying, Surly I will go down to Sheol in mourning to my son." (37:33,35). Jacob and his family had to endure a good portion of, "seven years of famine" (41:54). When Jacob thought he'd have to send Benlamin into Egypt, he said, "You have bereaved me of my children: Joseph is no more, and Simeon is no more, and you would take Benjamin. All these things are against me." (42:36).

But just here God surprised Jacob with the best news he could've possibly received: His beloved-son Joseph was alive, ruling Egypt and is plenty rich enough to take care of the entire family. Yes, ultimately, God has the best for all of His people! Joseph's brothers had sold him into slavery, and were afraid when he introduced himself. But Joseph, being spiritually aware, said, "It was not you who sent me here; but God!" (Genesis 45:8). Let us remember, when we are God's, no matter how things look, it is not people who are doing or saying to you--it is God!

Through all these trials, Jacob learned to love and trust God. The things he endured all had a purpose. At the end, he could see clearly in a spiritual way and even knew enough to give Joseph's younger son the best blessing over his older son (48:14). Jacob was so delivered from this world (represented by Egypt), that he made Joseph promise, "But when I lie down with my fathers, carry me out of Egypt and bury me in their burial place." ((47:30).

When Jacob blessed Joseph, just before he died, he looked back over his life and spoke of, "The God Who has been my Shepherd all my life to this day, the angel Who has redeemed me from all evil" (48:15-16). Speaking of this moment, Hebrews 11:21 says, Jacob "worshiped, leaning on the top of his staff." Yes, he worshiped, leaning on the very staff he used because he walked with a limp! If God has touched you in such a way as to cause a limitation of sorts (a limp)--praise Him! Oh that we all may, at long-last, have at least one moment when we give God pure heart-felt worship!

May it be said of us, "In the grace of God we have conducted ourselves in the world" (2 Cor, 1:12). "Be patient with everyone." (1 Thess. 5:14).

Printed in the United States
by Baker & Taylor Publisher Services